IT'S HARD SELLING JUST ONE TRUCK TO THIS MAN.

Published by Bob Tuck
Low Worsall. Yarm,
North Yorkshire, England TS15 9QA

ISBN   0 9521938 7 6

First published 2006
Copyright 2006 Bob Tuck

Other books by Bob Tuck:

Moving Mountains
Mountain Movers
Mammoth Trucks
Hauling Heavyweights
The Supertrucks of Scammell
Move It (Compendium of *Moving Mountains*
And *Mountain Movers*)
Carrying Cargo
Classic Hauliers
Robsons
Classic Hauliers 2
The Golden Days of Heavy Haulage
A Road Transport Heritage
A Road Transport Heritage Vol II
A Road Transport Heritage Vol III
100 Years of Heavy Haulage
Trucks (reprint of *Mammoth Trucks*)
King of the Road
Hills of Botley
Ritchies of Hetton-le-Hole

Printed in Great Britain by
Amadeus Press Ltd
Cleckheaton,
West Yorkshire BD19 4TQ

Typesetting by Highlight Type Bureau Ltd
Bradford, West Yorkshire BD8 7BY

Book design by
Sylbert Productions
Pavey Ark.

Front Cover and previous page: With a life span lasting over 78 years, the image of Donald Malcolm went through many changes. However, those that knew him best will certainly be able to relate to the portrayal on the front cover; 'Why have one telephone conversation when – at the same time - you can have two,' Donald would no doubt comment in the days when the concept of telephone conferencing calls was yet to be invented. To a man who loved to keep his finger on the pulse and loved to keep in touch with friends, family and work colleagues, the telephone was Donald's most favoured aid. Jerry Young took this photograph in July 1987 for use in a feature for *Truck* magazine.

A Seddon Atkinson photographer took the other shot in 1978 but Donald's rather fierce expression is a one seen by many truck salesmen who knocked on his office door. The Seddon Atkinson visit was to mark the sale of 18 Sed Atk 300 six wheel tippers although in service, these weren't the most successful of vehicles ever operated by Malcolms.

Rear Cover: With the stunning back drop of the 3,194' high mass of Ben Lomond virtually on your doorstep, there's no wonder that a favoured location for that special Malcolm photograph is often to be found on this part of Loch Lomond. The Burnbrae Road based Volvo FH12 L037 now bears the registration of SG 52 OGX.

Front and rear end papers: PM Photography is based in Burford Road, Camberley, Surrey, which must be at least 450 miles away from Brookfield. However, his extensive knowledge (and many years of experience) allows photographer Phil Moth, to speak for the many UK road transport enthusiasts who share a high regard for the WH Malcolm operation: 'I've always had a soft spot for this company because the attractive traditional style of livery on their vehicles means they always appear so well turned out. And with such a lengthy history, it's like seeing an old friend when one comes along.' In supplying all the PM photographs used for the two displays (inside the front & back covers) Phil asks that credit is also given to North Yorkshire based Colin Wright who took quite a lot of the shots over the years.

Contents

Author's Acknowledgements

With the gift of hindsight, it's obvious that research on this book should have started about 10 years ago. Had Donald been able to document all of his thoughts and experiences then the wealth of material could have surely filled a series of books. However, as that hasn't been possible, I've relied on many people recalling just a few of their thoughts on this very special man.

It is Donald's sister Morag who recalled the earliest days at Brookfield while the memories of Donald's wife Wilma go back to the times when WH Malcolm was very much in its infancy. The brothers Andrew and Walter Malcolm recalled their earliest memories while many early members of staff – past & present - were pleased to recall their involvement with Donald. These include Jim H. Anderson, Alex Brodie, Bert Brown, John Douglas, Robert English, Tom Hamilton, Hughie Hastie, Billy Kirkpatrick, Jack Love, James McGlynn, Dave McLune, John Melrose, Bob Monaghan, Frank Murney, Jimmy Paterson, George Scott, Charles Stewart, Peter Strachan and John Wilson. Sadly Willie Ballantyne is not still with us to read about his recollections.

In order to allow even more specific – and personal - memories of Donald to be printed, those contributing to the section 'I remember Donald,' are also thanked. Bill Hughes – regarding Grampian – and Bill Lind, relating to Loanhead Transport, are also thanked for their contributions. While I also want to thank good friend Jack Semple (now on *Motor Transport* but previously with *Truck* magazine) for his recollections and also allowing the use of the cover photograph.

Although the company has a huge amount of archives, many of the photographs used in this book have been sourced by friends – and fellow road transport enthusiasts - who have given me all sorts of assistance with many of my books in the past. Thanks again go to Andrew Burton, Andy Keith, Malcolm Mortimore, Phil Moth, Bill Reid and Dave Weston. And many thanks also to Andy Salter (of *Commercial Motor*) Malcolm Wilford and – king of the fleet lists – John Mollett for access to their fastidious records & archives.

Regarding the physical logistics of putting the book together, I have to thank many folk in the Malcolm Group for their time and consideration. Anne Lyall has been the very patient, chief gofer while help also came from Roz Reid (now in Canada) Alan Linklater plus IT specialist Gordon McCrorie. While helping with caption details were John Boal, Trevor Booth, Eddie Cunningham, Sandy Deans, Jimmy Donnelly, Tony English, John Holwell, Gordon Lauder, Gordon Lawns, Freddie McAllister, Gordon McDonald, and George McTaggart. Plus a special mention for Fiona Malcolm.

The early details on Brookfield village have been taken from the excellent publication: 'A Short History of Brookfield 1896-2001,' by Tom Dunn and Bryan Wylie.

My wife Sylvia continues to be a huge guide and help but of course the physical condition of this book is again down to the combined efforts of the Highlight Type Bureau and Amadeus Press. With particular thanks going to Angela Swaine and Steve Waddington (for their personal input & huge consideration) plus the continued support of another good friend, Richard Cook.

I was never fortunate enough to meet Donald Malcolm but in researching a book of this nature, it quickly became apparent how many lives he touched on – for the better. It's hoped that this account of his life goes a small way in placing that involvement on the record.

Low Worsall
North Yorks

May 2006.

Foreword

by
Andrew Malcolm

I knew Dad under various guises – a father, a grandfather, a boss, a businessman and a bloody nuisance, but most importantly, probably the closest friend I had.

As a father with a son like me, who wanted to do everything with him, he always allowed me to go with him and the amount I learned, the awe with which I held him and the respect I had for his knowledge, he will never have known.

Son, he always used to say to me, don't forget in life the most important asset, is people and everyone who worked for Dad didn't work for Donald Malcolm, they worked with Donald Malcolm.

As a bloody nuisance, he would drive somewhere when he wasn't supposed to, change my plans and get his tippers painted first in the paint shop.

No one person influenced my life greater than Dad and although obviously not to the same extent, many families' lives were influenced by Donald Malcolm. The decisions he made gave them long-term employment, stability, in some cases for more than one member of the family and gave them a job & a company to be proud of. With pictures of him all about the various depots, I still wonder when making my decisions whether he would have approved of them, but hopefully he would and no matter, he would have supported them in full.

A character certainly, a legend maybe, a successful businessman, undoubtedly, but to me a loving father, always missed.

He was in business a well kent and respected figure in the West of Scotland. His word was his bond and his handshake enough to secure any deal. Although he was happy to portray himself as big, loud and bossy – a man with a kinder heart and deeper emotions you couldn't meet. The amazing loyalty and respect he obtained from suppliers, customers and employees, was down to the quieter, smaller and unheralded words of comfort or acts of kindness that he was so often involved in.

His strongest interest in life was in people and he liked nothing better than knowing your mother, grandmother or uncle and discussing incidents and memories that he had of them.

After Dad died so many people came up with stories and memories of him that I thought why not have a permanent reminder of these stories and write a book – the final creation is now here. Hopefully this book will be enjoyed by vehicle enthusiasts, employees, ex-employees and friends and will act as a permanent history not only of Donald Malcolm but also of the Malcolm haulage story.

In reading it, you certainly get a feeling for the company and the man, how both were undoubtedly interlinked and how from the early beginnings, a large and successful company has emerged. Dad's humour and the stories shine through and I am sure everyone who picks the book up will find that it not only brings back a few memories of their own, but also gives them a few hours of enjoyment and laughter. Could I thank everyone who has contributed to this book and especially, Bob Tuck who has collated everyone's thoughts and brought them together in a publication that I am sure Dad would love to have read – I can imagine his comments.

Brookfield

May 2006.

With Walter Malcolm dying prematurely in 1934 when his family were still very young, not many group photographs were ever taken. This one dates from around 1930 and sees Donald in the centre while his parents – Walter and Marion – are supporting his two younger sisters Morag and Agnes.

About 65 years later, Donald and his wife Wilma share this family picture with their two daughters – Wilma (on the right) and Marion – with Andrew (on the left) and Walter.

THE MALCOLM FAMILY

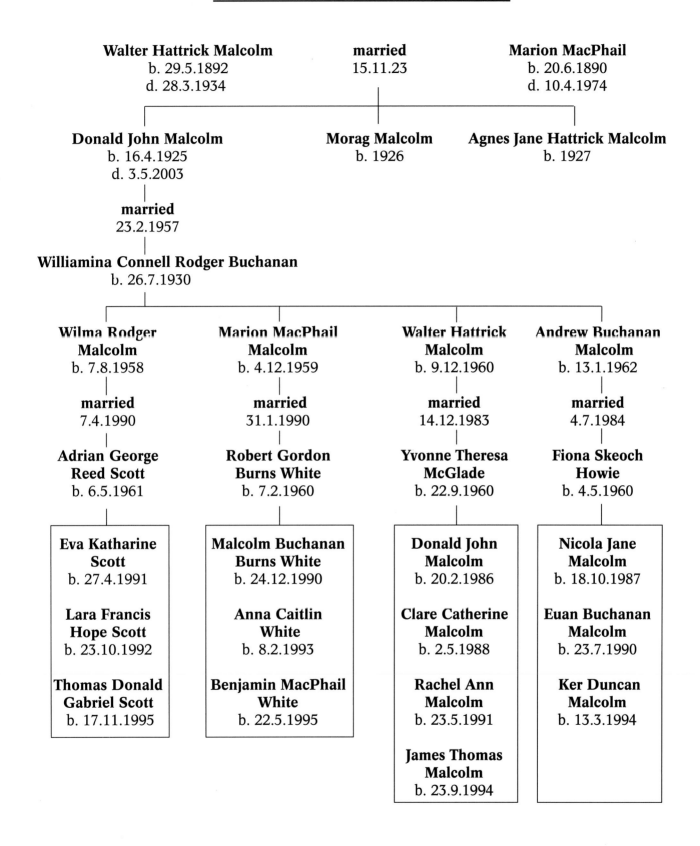

Walter Hattrick Malcolm
b. 29.5.1892
d. 28.3.1934

married
15.11.23

Marion MacPhail
b. 20.6.1890
d. 10.4.1974

Donald John Malcolm
b. 16.4.1925
d. 3.5.2003

Morag Malcolm
b. 1926

Agnes Jane Hattrick Malcolm
b. 1927

married
23.2.1957

Williamina Connell Rodger Buchanan
b. 26.7.1930

Wilma Rodger Malcolm
b. 7.8.1958

Marion MacPhail Malcolm
b. 4.12.1959

Walter Hattrick Malcolm
b. 9.12.1960

Andrew Buchanan Malcolm
b. 13.1.1962

married
7.4.1990

married
31.1.1990

married
14.12.1983

married
4.7.1984

Adrian George Reed Scott
b. 6.5.1961

Robert Gordon Burns White
b. 7.2.1960

Yvonne Theresa McGlade
b. 22.9.1960

Fiona Skeoch Howie
b. 4.5.1960

Eva Katharine Scott
b. 27.4.1991

Lara Francis Hope Scott
b. 23.10.1992

Thomas Donald Gabriel Scott
b. 17.11.1995

Malcolm Buchanan Burns White
b. 24.12.1990

Anna Caitlin White
b. 8.2.1993

Benjamin MacPhail White
b. 22.5.1995

Donald John Malcolm
b. 20.2.1986

Clare Catherine Malcolm
b. 2.5.1988

Rachel Ann Malcolm
b. 23.5.1991

James Thomas Malcolm
b. 23.9.1994

Nicola Jane Malcolm
b. 18.10.1987

Euan Buchanan Malcolm
b. 23.7.1990

Ker Duncan Malcolm
b. 13.3.1994

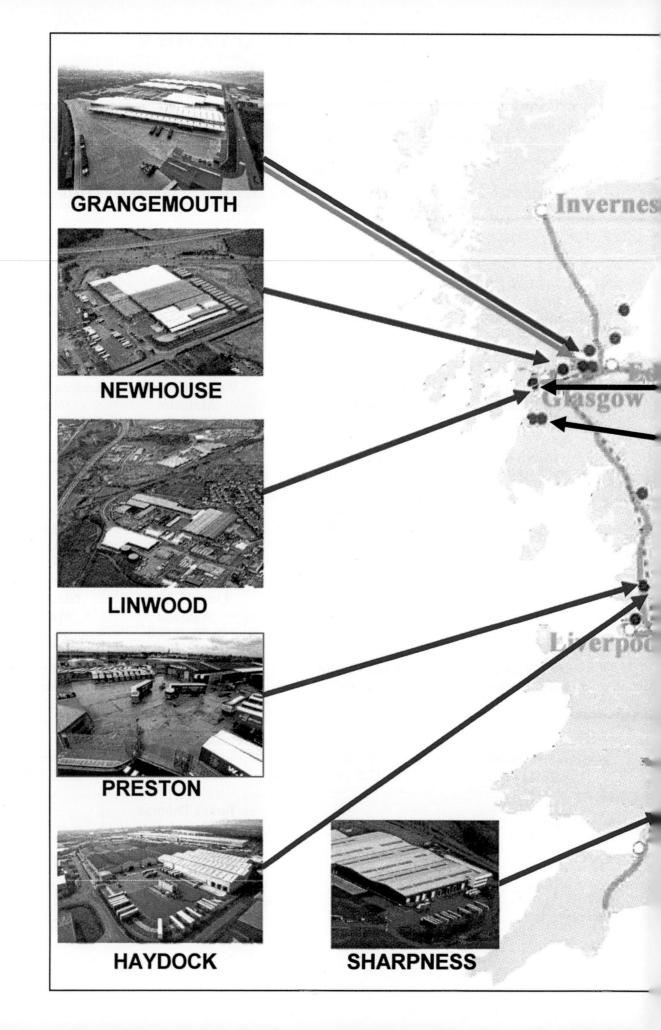

GRANGEMOUTH

NEWHOUSE

LINWOOD

PRESTON

HAYDOCK

SHARPNESS

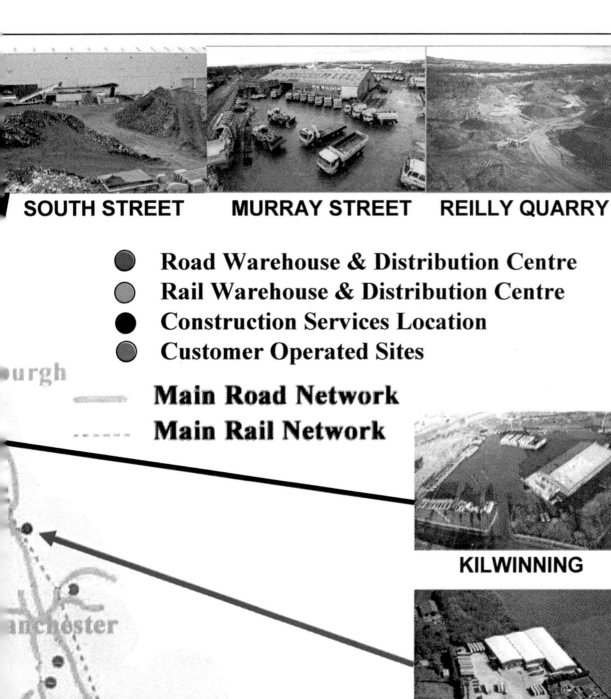

SOUTH STREET **MURRAY STREET** **REILLY QUARRY**

- Road Warehouse & Distribution Centre
- Rail Warehouse & Distribution Centre
- Construction Services Location
- Customer Operated Sites

— Main Road Network
... Main Rail Network

KILWINNING

GATENBY

The **MALCOLM** *Group*

www.malcolmgroup.co.uk

CRICK

This page and overleaf. The Malcolm Group is one of the big success stories to come out of Scotland. From a modest start in 1925, with a horse & cart, Walter Hattrick Malcolm laid the foundations of what must be one of the largest family owned concerns on the UK transport scene. With the mission slogan of 'Practical solutions, successful partnerships,' Malcolms are now considered invaluable by a huge number of blue chip concerns that trust them to handle their complete supply chain operation. The WH Malcolm historical roots come from the operation of tippers and their current diverse portfolio of machines and experienced manpower, means that Malcolm Construction Services is now regarded as a one stop shop contractor for civil engineering and groundwork services throughout central Scotland. Malcolms are the recognised leader in waste management, re-use and re-cycling of construction and demolition waste in Scotland. With seven fully licensed landfill sites in central and west Scotland, the company handles two million tonnes of material annually.

The Malcolm Way

Unique is something of an over used word, but when it comes to the transport world, describing the Malcolm Group as anything else doesn't seem to do it justice. Yes, there are many other concerns in Logistics but Malcolm's 310 strong road fleet based at 22 operational locations across the United Kingdom ensures they are a major player in Networking with British Industry. And if you add on in excess of 3 million square feet of warehousing plus the use of integrated rail freight solutions, you'll probably agree that Malcolms are something special – but their business doesn't stop there.

The stand alone Construction Services Division does everything from earthmoving to bulk excavations; building roads, car parks and even installing sports pitches. While their expertise in waste management covers both recycling and landfill. And currently, Malcolms operate more than 140 tippers plus another 140 items in their plant hire fleet – including the biggest low loaders necessary to move their diverse equipment.

Looking after all their machinery in house has long been part of the Malcolm brief but the Group's Maintenance Services Division now looks after all manner of vehicles and equipment for other people in transport whether they carry freight or people. The purpose built workshops at Linwood incorporates eight bays, five controlled environment spray paint booths, a tachograph fitting centre and a speed limiter centre – along with their own state of the art, private & commercial testing centre. While having their own recovery vehicles means they can collect vehicles, which cannot make it into the workshops under their own power.

Malcolms have long been committed to giving a superior customer service and to that end, for more than 40 years they've always had the support of being a major part of Grampian Holdings plc. That link ended however, on 25th May 2005 as the Malcolm Group came full circle when it came back into private ownership under Andrew and Walter Malcolm.

If all that doesn't make you believe that the Malcolm Group is unique then you're a difficult person to convince. But like any good argument, I've kept the strongest reason for the end.

There are currently more than 1,800 people on the Malcolm Group pay roll and while I didn't pick out 48 year old George Scott for any particular reason, as Centre Manager of the Maintenance Services Division, he can look back on an entire working life with the Malcolm Group: 'I suppose people like me are Malcolmised,' says George. You probably won't find that word in an English – or Scottish – dictionary but if you are one of those 1,800+ Malcolm workers, then you'll know exactly what George means - when you're one of the Malcolm team, you work in a particular fashion.

One man – Donald Malcolm - created that fashion and while Donald died on 3rd May 2003, the legacy he created still lives strongly on in both his family and the huge team he pulled together in driving the business on.

These few words were supposed to be an introduction to the Malcolm history and while you will read about horses and carts, tippers and trains and even holes in the ground, Donald Malcolm has touched upon virtually everything you will read about.

Donald lived and breathed the Malcolm Group business and its success was fuelled simply by the passion and drive he engendered in his family & staff. If you had the good fortune to meet with, work for – or even come into competition with – this big hulk of man, you'll agree that when the word unique was thought up, then Donald Malcolm was the presence which came to mind.

The Malcolm relationship with both Scania and Rockware Glass go back almost 40 years. Donald Malcolm was amongst the first Scottish buyers of the well-liked Scania Vabis tractor units, while the relationship with Rockware was established after the Kilwinning concern of William Kerr was taken over by Grampian in 1967 and absorbed into the WH Malcolm operation. The Rockware traffic of glass containers (all manner of bottles & jars) was first hauled out of the Portland works at Irvine but it wasn't long before the Malcolm vehicles were visiting the Rockware Knottingley and Doncaster plants.

It became a Malcolm trademark – which Donald always insisted on - that whenever any brand new vehicles were to be first registered, then it must have an HS – Renfrewshire County Council – number issued by the Paisley taxation office. However, when the vehicle registration system was overhauled in 2001, the new style of half yearly registration pattern didn't allow for the continuance of the HS link and a system of fleet numbering was adopted. Malcolm's plant vehicles have long had numbers (as they don't always carry registrations) but the company's Logistics (L) and Construction (C) vehicles now have their own prefixes. Trailers also carry fleet numbers generally with the prefix of H. This stood for Hustler, a specific model name of curtainsider trailer, although all curtainsiders now carry the letter H. The LH prefix is to denote a Hustler of a Lower height. As well as different makes of vehicle, the Malcolm maximum weight tractor units also vary from day cab units (which are generally double shifted) to standard sleeper cabs and double sleepers – depending on the work they do. The day cab ERF ECS L704 is a Newhouse based vehicle while the Renault Premium L742 – with sleeper cab - is Haydock based although pictured at Linwood in October 2004.

Based on a Renault Kerax 8x4 chassis, T236 RGA was referred to as the company's Brimec vehicle. The term indicates how the vehicle's body can slide back and angle itself down to the ground. However, the body wasn't built by Brimec but built in-house at WH Malcolm. When in service, it was the only one of its type also kitted out with a Hiab crane. With an unladen weight of around 16 tonnes, it was normally used for the transport of small items of plant. First driven by Ian McKendrick, it then had Andrew Dixon driving it for a while.

It became standard practice in the Malcolm Group that if there were other members of staff with the same name as you, then you were also given a number. So regular driver of Malcolm's 150 tonnes gross Scania 8x4 heavy hauler is described as Jim Russell 2. As the fleet number denotes, this outfit was originally part of the Burnbrae Road Logistics fleet, although the company's heaviest low loaders are now allocated to the Plant side of the group. The Scania's Nooteboom semi-trailer is loaded with a Volvo machine described as a 36 tonner, which gives the outfit a gross weight of around 100 tonnes.

The Malcolm Group's body building expertise also extends to making the bodies for the company's tippers. The Volvo FM12 8x4 chassis is considered to be a well liked, general-purpose tipper and currently there are about 44 of them in service, with SF 03 GAA being a Kilwinning based vehicle. Fitting capes – or greedy boards – to extend the sides upwards on the Malcolm tippers has been standard practice since the earliest of days so that a full load of a lighter cargo can be carried. The big difference to the Malcolm designed extension of the 21st century is that two, fork lift key holes are incorporated into the capes so putting these awkward lengths of steel on (or taking them off) is simplified.

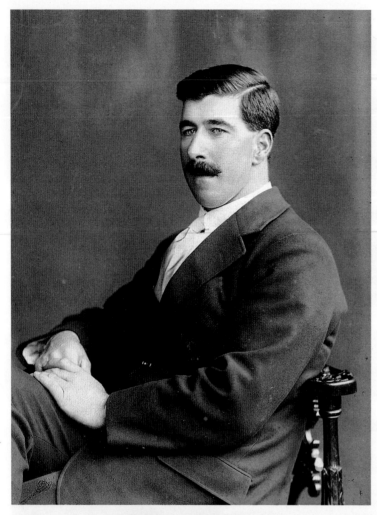

Walter Hattrick Malcolm (pictured left) was to give more than just his name to the WH Malcolm business, which he established in 1925. The hard work ethic was something he engendered and is perhaps, the main reason why the business achieved so much subsequent success. Deciding to make the move to Boghouse Farm at Brookfield (below) was also very significant although until they bought the property in 1942, initially, the Malcolms only rented the lower floor – and outbuildings - of the farmhouse. Although many changes have subsequently been made with Boghouse, the Malcolm mechanics of old will probably recall the large tree seen on the left. When any vehicle engines had to be lifted out, this tree was often used as an anchorage point for an overhead lifting mechanism. Donald and his sister Morag are seen in the driveway of the house around 1930.

CHAPTER 1

The Brook in a Field

Go to the village of Brookfield today and you're hard pushed to imagine what sort of transport history it has witnessed. This sleepy collection of up-market houses is only a mile or two – as the crow flies – from the Malcolm Group's current HQ at Burnbrae Drive in Linwood (amongst the south west suburbs of Glasgow) but in reality, it appears to be in a different time zone.

Brookfield (so named apparently when it was formed around 1896 as there was a small brook or stream running through a field) will always be the ancestral heart of the transport interests of WH Malcolm but the story of Donald John Malcolm doesn't start here. Donald's parents – Walter Hattrick Malcolm and Marion (nee McPhail) Malcolm - had married on 15th November 1923 and were living in a flat on Johnstone High Street when Donald was born on 16th April 1925.

While Walter was a native of the Johnstone area (his parents farmed Chapel Farm at Houston) Marion had been brought up in the village of Shawbost, on the Isle of Lewis' Atlantic coast.

There was very little in the way of employment on Lewis in the early 1900s – apart from weaving - so Marion had travelled south for work and went into service at Houston House before meeting up with Walter.

Even from their first meeting Walter was apparently smitten but Marion later recalled, she wasn't so sure. In order to test whether Walter was keen on her, Marion moved north to Invergarry – and waited to see what happened. And of course once Walter followed her up there, she declared: 'He's the man for me.'

When Donald was only four weeks old, Walter and Marion decided to move the mile or so from Johnstone to rent Boghouse Farm in Brookfield. They may not have realised what sort of huge business empire would spawn from this lovely house (with an awful sounding name) but what Walter did realise was the premises would be an ideal base for his fledgling coal round business.

Paying an annual rent of £46 to the owner – Peter Kerr – the Malcolm family took over the ground floor of the farmhouse. The upper floor was occupied by Mrs Hatrick (the previous owner of the house before Peter Kerr bought it) and her niece Miss Mary White. While the farmhouse garden was let to Mrs Hatrick, the Malcolms had use of a variety of outbuildings including barns, a byre, dairy, stable, and cart shed. There were also nine acres of land (the Malcolms did keep a small number of cows for their own use) but as part of the rental terms, Walter agreed to allow the Brookfield Ladies hockey team to train and play in the playing field during the winter months.

HARD WORK

Anyone who has ever contemplated working for the Malcolm organisation has always been under no misapprehension that they are signing up to work hard. Back in the late 1920s, Walter did nothing else and neither did his wife Marion as she soon had two more young children – daughters Morag (the Gaelic version of Marion) and Agnes – to look after. And as soon as young Donald grew old enough to pick up a shovel, he adopted the hard work ethic into a Malcolm trait and in truth, it's the simple reason behind the family's subsequent business success.

The Malcolm domestic coal round of the period involved shovelling coal out of the rail trucks at Johnstone North railway station and then loading that coal into individual sacks of 1cwt per time. Transporting those sacks – by horse & cart – before delivering the fuel into all manner of strangely located coal houses – six days a week – was physically very demanding but Walter couldn't relax about having a captive

The village of Brookfield was only created following the vision of Peter Kerr – a civil engineer / architect - when he bought Boghouse Farm in the mid 1890s. The thriving industrial success of nearby Johnstone – coupled with the adjacent excellent railway links to Paisley, Greenock and Glasgow – was to make Brookfield an ideal upmarket, dormitory village. There are records of the existence of Boghouse as far back as the 1600s although as well as building houses on the farmland, Peter Kerr also improved the access to Boghouse after the village road network of Victoria Road, Albert Road, Woodside Road and Stanley Drive was made. Walter Malcolm came from farming stock and although he did keep some cattle at Boghouse, these were simply for the family's own use. As these early pictures from the Malcolm family album portray, growing up at Boghouse must have been a wonderful experience for the young Malcolm family. Donald (pictured adopting the same calf holding pose as his father) formed a great affinity with the farming community and kept those forged links until the day he died.

market as he was in competition with Wilsons, another merchant based at Johnstone North station. Two Clydesdale horses – a white one named 'Charlie' and one brown - were to be the first Malcolm traction and at first things went fairly well.

Sunday was of course a day of rest and after walking to the local Church at Houston to hear Reverend Muir, a treat for the whole Malcolm family was to visit Walter's sister – Jessie - who lived on Lambridden Farm. Taking the bus to Dalry, it still meant for a long walk – of at least a mile – but Donald's young sister Morag fondly remembers these visits.

However, no matter how hard you work, sometimes life can come along and kick you in the teeth. And even though Walter Malcolm looked a fit, tall, dark haired strapping guy, he was to suffer with digestive problems. Naturally, as time allowed, he'd seek medical advice but no one apparently anticipated that when Walter was taken into the Western Infirmary in Glasgow, he would actually die there (on 28th March 1934 at the age of 42) due to complications after an ulcer perforated.

It's almost impossible to imagine what Marion Malcolm – and her three children - felt like at that time. However, with those three small children all under the age of nine, her response was to simply work even harder. She didn't contemplate giving up the WH Malcolm coal round (because it was the family's only source of income) but much needed help to keep the business going was to come in the form of Donald McIver. He originated from Marion's home Isle of Lewis but came to Johnstone and oversaw the Malcolm operation from a small hut at the town's North station. But as time was to tell, the eventual saviour of the WH Malcolm business was already in the Malcolm household even though – at 8 years old – he wasn't yet aware of it.

The horse & cart may seem a very old fashioned method of transport (in the 21st century) but it's probably one of the most efficient door to door, modes of haulage when you have a good Clydesdale horse like Charlie involved. Walter Malcolm is holding the reins whilst in Thompson Street, Johnstone. Even when Malcolms joined the mechanised age (in 1930 when they bought their first Morris 30cwt load carrier) they retained the use of horse pulled traction until the mid 1940s. Donald proved adept enough in being to handle both these modes of horse power.

Seen in the centre of the back row, Donald may have stood out as being much taller than his similar age classmates in this Kilbarchan Primary school photograph. But subsequently leaving the John Neilson school at Paisley when only 13 was still a huge step for him to take. Donald had rode with the Malcolm drivers as often as schooling allowed and his legs soon grew out of his early overalls. Malcolm's first mechanised load carrier was a Morris 30cwt and was bought in 1930. HS 7555 dates new from around 1934 although sadly none of the Leyland Cub archives have survived. The model was built at Leyland's Kingston-on-Thames factory and described as a lightweight 2-3 tonner. It's imagined this latter part of the maker's specification was never adhered to at Brookfield. Also not known is the name of the Malcolm driver. Morag Malcolm recalls some of the early drivers as: Willie Blackwood, Jimmy Quinn, John Allison, Jimmy Young, Jimmy Murney and Charlie Galbraith.

CHAPTER 2

Life Begins at 13

Walter Malcolm had joined the mechanised age in 1930 when their first Morris 30cwt four-wheeler was bought for the sum of £150. Not a lot of money today but it was quite a price – then – for a second hand vehicle and the transaction was only possible because Marion was able to borrow the £35 down payment from a friend. The horses stayed in use (until the mid 1940s) and it was business as usual as for the next 20 years, the coal round remained an important part of the Malcolm workload. Something else, which has always been an important part to Malcolms, is their attitude to man management. Back in 1934 it just seemed common sense for Marion Malcolm to look after the staff even though, it meant walking the mile into Johnstone every day with a flask of tea and sandwiches for the men. And when the wagon came back to Boghouse on a night and any repairs were required, the drivers knew that one of the Malcolm family would be over to the garage with tea and food to keep them going, for as long as it took to get the vehicle roadworthy again for the next day. And they also knew they'd get paid overtime until the job was finished.

To Donald Malcolm, getting involved in the coal round was something he'd always wanted to do. As a youngster, he'd attended Kilbarchan Primary School before moving on to the John Neilson School in Paisley. But really, all his spare time was spent with those first coal drivers learning about the route, the customers and the mechanics of the vehicle. Donald would often collect the coal round money from the houses they were delivering to and it's perhaps no surprise that Donald could change a wheel on those first Malcolm coal lorries, long before he left school.

WAR TIME EFFORT

In the 1930s, it was normal to allow children to leave school at the age of 14 – if they weren't seeking higher education. Donald Malcolm knew exactly the form of further education he required and even though he was still 13, he was allowed to leave school so he could become involved – full time – in the family business.

A life long friend of Donald was Cochrane McLeod who recalled: 'Donald never took school too seriously although he was always good fun. He wasn't interested in sport although might play in goal at football. But really, even at that time, you could see how focussed he was on helping his Mother make the business a success.'

In early 1939 the focus of the entire country was in what was happening on the other side of the English Channel as the threat of World War II grew ever closer. That was too far away for young Donald to worry about, as he was more concerned in learning how to drive the coal wagon. Of course, his sister Morag stresses that Donald never drove on the public roads until he was 17 and if you have heard to the contrary, then you must be mistaken. That was the excuse given to the local policeman in Johnstone when he later thought he saw Donald driving (many times) but in fairness, just getting people able to drive the coal wagon was a major concern once men – and women – were signing up for service in the Armed Forces.

It helped to confuse the authorities that Donald was a big strapping lad when compared to many others. Apparently one day when he drove the wagon into the yard, Marion Malcolm asked her son who was the 'wee boy' that was riding with him. That wee boy was actually a fellow haulage contractor – Danny McColgan – who was showing Donald how to drive even though he was head & shoulders smaller than 'Young' Donald.

At first, Donald was too young to serve in the Armed Services and as the war progressed, he

FHS 455 was new in 1952 and like many of Malcolm's Austin pickups was used for a variety of roles. Hughie Hastie recalls using them for breakdowns although Bob Monoghan recalls how they were also his ride to and from work: 'One of the drivers, Willie Arthur, was entrusted to take one of the pickups home but about eight or nine of us could also squeeze onboard. He would also pick us up about 6am the following day.'

The Dodge four-wheel tipper DHS 64 – seen with Donald and neighbour Ruth Snodgrass - was new in June 1947. A search of the Renfrewshire taxation records (by Malcolm Wilford) reveals that over the next two years, Malcolms were to register 12 more vehicles, with DHS prefixes: 278, 339, 435, 498, 603, 645, 717, 740, 805, 909, 989. Not all of these were brand new

as Malcolms bought two, ex Army Canadian Ford 4x4s which Willie Ballantyne and John McDade drove. As seen in the lower shot, Malcolms used them to get into places, where most tippers didn't like to go. Although there were two of these Fords, there was only one set of clip on, Perspex windows – and whichever driver got in first to work, then he would grab the windows. While the fate of the Ford is unknown, the Dodge – DHS 64 - ended its days as a skip for all the waste scrap metal generated around the yard. But when the scrap man Tommy Houston eventually towed it away, it wasn't realised the power take off was still engaged. So as he pulled the vehicle, the tipper was raised and all the scrap was tipped off.

became too invaluable to the local transport scene so was exempted from National Service. Hard to believe that one youngster could make such an impression but in truth, during the wartime years, young people grew up very quickly – they had to.

The war effort saw Malcolms involved in all manner of activities and they were allowed to do this, because of rapid expansion: 'By 1946, the fleet had increased five-fold,' Donald Malcolm later recalled, 'I then had five vehicles.' Those early vehicles were of diverse make with Austin, Bedford and Canadian built Fords being bought. All were tippers, even though some of the time they may be carrying Prisoners-of-War from the local detention camps prior to them being put to work.

A lot of the essential Malcolm wartime work was sourced from the nearby Royal Ordnance Factory at Bishopton and at times, use of the Malcolm tippers was required 24 hours a day. Literally hundreds of people had worked there mainly producing shells and armaments although with most of the Bishopton complex being underground, not everyone knew everything that went on there.

It was quite legal for Donald to drive off the public road – in private complexes like Bishopton – and of course there was no age limit on driving a horse and cart. Bob Monaghan (who comes into the Malcolm story slightly later) recalls regularly seeing Donald delivering coal with a horse and a two wheeled cart: 'During the War, I'll always remember Donald as wearing a flat cap – but always at a jaunty angle.'

The various mills in Johnstone were serviced by Malcolm's coal business and Bob recalls even in those early days how Donald would get extra coal into the cart by building the sides up using a set of greedy boards. Although the cart was loaded by hand, unloading was simply done by releasing a spring catch, which allowed the cart body to rotate and tip itself. 'Although Donald had to walk alongside the cart when he was loaded,' says Bob, 'when he was empty, he'd take off one of the greedy boards and sit on that – astride the cart - as he rode back for another load.'

Although this was a serious time, it didn't stop humour altogether and Donald found himself the butt of one particular practical joke. It was sheer hard work transhipping the coal from the railway trucks into the Malcolm tipper but long before the days of mechanised loaders, it was something you just had to do. Young Donald was quicker than most because he could make lightening use of the biggest size 12 shovel and bent his back well into the task. But, one day, as the coal truck's heap descended – so Donald was out of sight from his tipper – some so called friends decided to slow young Malcolm down a bit. In creeping forward (while shielded by the railway truck) they could lean into the wagon's cab and release the handbrake so they could push the tipper forward a bit. Donald didn't realise this as he was too busy shovelling away but when he realised the ejected coal was taking too long to make its landing noise, he looked over the side of the truck. He then discovered there was a heap of coal on the roadway as his motor had been pushed out the way. The incident prompted Donald to chase after his so called mates who got the wrath of his temper. Although as the Malcolm story progresses, this wouldn't be the last time Donald's voice would be raised.

MUSIC AND DANCE

Those who knew Donald will tell you he had several passions in his life. His family and business – obviously – were always his biggest loves but as a young man, he loved the sound of Scottish music and he also loved to dance. He always retained a long-term affinity with the local farming community and even when he died, he was still the Honorary President of the West Renfrewshire Young Farmer's Club.

After the War, Donald had always tried to attend as many Young Farmers dances in the area as he could. True he didn't have the daintiest feet around but he was always one of the first to get onto the dance floor. To those who recall big Donald as a man's man, the guy himself would have been the first to acknowledge that he owed a great deal to the many women who came into his life.

First and foremost he has his mother Marion to thank not only for bringing him up – in the hardest of times – but also for being a guide and confidant as the fledgling Malcolm business grew. Some people might say that Marion of course spoiled her only son although as Donald worked so hard, he probably merited a bit of special attention. Donald's two sisters Morag & Agnes were also a big part of his life while in 1950, Donald was to meet perhaps the biggest influence in his life when he first danced with Wilma Buchanan. 'I think it was Donald's nice nature which first attracted me to him,' recalls Wilma, 'as he was so big, cuddly and affectionate.'

Wilma wasn't the only girl Donald danced with but the chance to have a longer talk with Donald – away from the dance floor – cropped up because of Donald leaving his coat behind: 'I was Secretary of the Young Farmers at the time and when I discovered he'd left his coat at a dance in Kilmarnock, I said I would let him have it back. It seemed a good way of getting to know him better.' However, Wilma says, the biggest influence on winning big Donald's heart was to be the cooking of her mother (who was also called Wilma). 'We farmed at Linhead Farm, Uplawmoor near Dunlop,' says Wilma, 'and once

Donald walked into our parlour and smelt what my mother was cooking in the oven, it certainly broke the ice.'

Donald may have soon got his feet under the Buchanan table although the courtship of Wilma was something that wasn't rushed. Simply finding the time to get together was often difficult as Donald poured all his efforts into expanding the Malcolm business. In total, Donald & Wilma spent seven years getting to know each other before their marriage in 1957. While the following 46 years was to prove anything but uneventful, even the honeymoon is something, which Wilma Malcolm will never forget.

Logan, Sons & Co. were a big coal merchant in Paisley and Malcolms had two of these BMC / Austin 7 ton tippers (which date new from 1956-57) painted in their contract livery. All the Malcolm sign writing (including the tartan) of the period was done by the talented Johnny Johnstone. Bob Monoghan recalls driving one of these first BMC diesel powered ones and recalls Roddy Nicholson as another regular driver. Although used normally on coal, two of the Austins ran on the Machrihanish job: 'I remember one breaking down on a Saturday afternoon at Campbeltown so Donald sent me out with the low loader to bring it back,' recalls the hard working Bob Monoghan.

When compared to its modern day counterparts, this Bray loading shovel (with a 15cwt – 1 ton capacity) looks particularly basic. However to many of the early Malcolm drivers – who were used to loading themselves by backbreaking shovel – the Bray was positively heaven sent. Seen on 24th March 1952, Jimmy Bright (who had the nickname 'Omo' – a famous soap powder of the time) is moving coal at the large Hillington terminal. Howard Nunnick's research reveals the Bray machine was manufactured in the southeast of England. Generally based on the Fordson Major tractor of the time, Bray would replace the Ford's original front axle – with a stronger version – when adding their lifting equipment.

Supplied to WH Malcolm in 1957 by Milburn Motors Ltd., this Albion Reiver PF107T was dedicated to carrying foam slag – a bi-product of the steel making industry. The material has been described by Malcolm men of old as more akin to pop corn or cornflakes, as it was very light but was a regular traffic for many tippers as far north as Dyce near Aberdeen. But even with such high sides, the Malcolm tippers would hardly carry more than 4 tons in weight. George Mason is recalled as being the regular driver of this Albion, which sports Milburn built bodywork. It's not known if George was driving on the day when this Albion turned over on itself but so light was the material – and so sturdy the motor – that when it was righted, there was very little damage.

It was a big day at Boghouse in the mid 1950s when the McKeachan builders from Houston came and erected the new garage although before that, the Malcolm staff had to demolish two large Nissen huts, which had been occupying the ground. The lean-to building on the right side of the garage was then the vehicle stores while the large building behind was used to park vehicles in overnight. Bob Monoghan recalled that on a Saturday afternoon – like a Sergeant Major - Donald insisted they were always lined up inside, just right: 'But on a Monday morning it was bedlam – just like the start of the Le Mans race.' Donald – and neighbour Ruth Snodgrass - is pictured with his Ford Prefect car wearing his cap at its normal jaunty angle. The Bedford coal wagon to the right of the garage was normally driven by John Gilmour while the Chaseside loading shovel – inside the garage – was new in 1956.

27

The WH Malcolm transport concern was too modest – and localised – to be effected by the phase of Nationalisation which effected many road hauliers between 1948-1951. However, in 1950, Donald decided to give up his coal round business and concentrate on contracting. This didn't just mean tipper work as flat vehicles were also operated. To broaden the scope of the Malcolm operation, various licences – and their vehicles – were bought. These included the purchase of four Special 'A' licences – in February 1954 – when British Road Services was being partially de-nationalised. The Albion Clydesdale FHS 498 dates new from 1952 and was normally driven by Duncan McCormack. Distillery work took him as far north as Dufftown and as far south as Ayrshire.

Malcolm's first earth moving machine – a Caterpillar 955 - was bought in 1955 although this 977H was new in 1962. The USA built machine tipped the scales around the 16 tons mark and had a 2.5 cubic yard capacity bucket. It was versatile enough to handle a variety of materials, its operator being John 'Jock' Smith. Certain tracked shovels and excavators were registered by Malcolms, which made it legal for them to travel – under their own power – along the road for short distances.

CHAPTER 3

Marriage and Macrihanish

As the country was slowly re-building itself from the war time years of deprivation, the Glasgow area was a booming pulse in the UK's industrial infrastructure. Many involved in long distance general haulage had seen their activities heavily curtailed - while some transport companies disappeared entirely as the late 1940s Labour Government's dictate of compulsory purchase (Nationalisation) saw these concerns bought up and repainted into the colours of British Road Services.

Malcolm's local work wasn't touched however and with so many building projects being started in the area, the prospect of expansion shone its light on Brookfield. While Donald was as keen as mustard to expand and buy up other people's vehicles - plus their vital carriers licences – which became available, Marion wanted to take things a bit slower. However, as the 1950s progressed, the smaller firms of Allardyce of Linwood, McNeil of Renfrew, McDonald of Scotstoun & Kelvin Transport were bought out and the WH Malcolm fleet grew ever larger.

In 1950, the domestic coal merchant business was sold on although moving coal remained a regular part of the Malcolm workload. When Bob Monoghan joined WH Malcolm in 1952, his first job of the day (with his petrol engine Bedford four wheel tipper) was always to run into Johnstone North station and load – by hand operated shovel – two 6-7 ton loads of coal for different mills in Johnstone: 'With those loads done, I'd run into Babcock & Wilcox in Renfrew and spend the day working out of there carrying things like ash.'

Bob remained at Malcolms for about 25 years, however, at the start of his service – like many other Malcolm drivers then employed - he left and rejoined several times: 'Donald would blow up and sack me for something or other,' recalls Bob, 'or I'd get sick of things and just pack in. I normally went to Wilsons who were in competition with Malcolms but Donald would soon ask me back. However we eventually both agreed on a truce that I wouldn't chuck it again and Donald wouldn't sack me any more. But even now (more than 50 years later) I reckon Donald Malcolm was the greatest man I ever worked for. He never asked you to do anything he wouldn't do himself and he paid well.'

OFFICE STAFF

As the Malcolm fleet expanded, so did the need for more office staff. Mrs Jean Muirhead was one of the company's first typists although coming in 1952 to take over traffic office duties was Bert Brown: 'At the time I was working for the Leggat building & civil engineering concern – who had used Donald's tippers at times – and Donald asked if I'd come and work for him. I was ready for a change of job although I didn't realise how big a change it was going to be - I think I was working eight days a week when I was with Donald.'

Bert actually stayed for the next 38 years and was made a Director of WH Malcolm Ltd in 1962. His early days are recalled for not only having to sort out the traffic desk but also the drivers: 'I'd sometimes start as early as 6am to make sure everyone knew what they were doing, but I've also seen me go and knock up drivers who had slept in or just felt like a lie in. The bottom line with Donald was to make sure everyone was kept working for as many hours as legally possible. And if a job finished at say 3pm, I always had to find something else to do to fill the day in. There was no such thing as an early finish at Malcolms.'

About 1955, Marion Malcolm moved out of Boghouse Farm to live just a short distance away from the transport yard at 9 Victoria Road in a house she was soon to name 'Shawbost'. She sensed it wouldn't be long before Donald would want to bring his future wife to live at Boghouse and giving him the space made timing of that decision much easier. Two years would elapse before that happened although Donald's sister Morag stayed with him at first because of course someone was needed to look after the house. However it did help the Malcolm business that Marion was a short distance away from the haulage depot because she proved to be a saviour in the times when Donald's temper flared up.

Those who knew Donald will tell you that he may have had a quick temper but once he'd said his piece, then it was simply forgotten about. The big problem to the eruptions were encountered when he'd given one of his staff their marching orders – and told them never to come back. Because once they'd walked out of the Boghouse office with their employment (National Insurance) cards, it was at times an action that Donald would regret. He then had the chance to ring his mother up or Marion may even have sensed what was happening and may be waiting ready for a chat to whoever was making that walk away for the early 1 penny bus ride back into Johnstone. And – as you've guessed it – the subsiding of Donald's wrath often meant the sacked member was reinstated, long before they had left Brookfield. This is obviously no way to run a business in the 21st century (with all the employment regulations now in force) but if anything, it underlines the passionate drive, which Donald always had for the Malcolm business.

SUB CONTRACT

The WH Malcolm attitude to taking work on has long been that you never said you couldn't do it. Even when he only had five wagons, Donald would take on work for possibly twice that number and then use sub contractors to take up the slack. It often happened in the fetch and carry trade that some jobs would go off quicker than anticipated, so the vehicles could then be allocated to something else. Imagine that you are juggling a hot potato, then you have some idea of the situation Donald Malcolm regularly lived with but – of course – he had hands that were heat resistant. And once Bert Brown got responsible for the traffic desk, he shared the job of keeping all the hot potatoes in the air.

William Lind & Co were a large quarrying concern from Elderslie and while they operated their own fleet of tippers, when Donald first knocked at their door, it was to see if he could make use of the Lind vehicles – for his own work. Strange, you might say but Donald never let convention get in the way of things and in the late 1940s, the work he'd taken on at Greenock Tunnel West Station was more than his motors could handle.

One of the many good things that grew from the Malcolm – Lind connection was meeting Jack Love. Jack was to work for the Lind concern for 29 years but once he'd bought a house in Brookfield in 1954, the link to Donald became more than just a business relationship: 'Donald was very close to his mother,' recalls Jack, 'but I suppose he looked on me as someone else to discuss the things he was worried about. And living so close to the depot meant it was handy if he wanted to just call in.'

Jack Love was to eventually join the Malcolm management full time (after leaving the Lind concern in 1967) and was to stay with the company until he eventually retired at the age of 80 – yes, you did read that right. But while the upper tiers of any company are important, it should be stressed that folk like Hughie Hastie are just as much an integral part of the Malcolm success.

KINDNESS

In 1946, Donald was running five vehicles but 15 years later, the Malcolms of Brookfield operation had increased by more than 700% - when there were 37 vehicles in service. And as a reflection of how much the business was changing, by 1960 WH Malcolm were also operating seven earth-moving machines with Chaseside, International and Caterpillar being amongst the diverse makes bought.

The first wheeled mechanical shovel had appeared in 1951 as the company turned to answering the demands of the construction industry as their staple employment. Carrying coal – in bulk – to works or mills was still a major activity as were loads of ash from the local power stations, stone from the quarries or just loads of rubbish to the tip. If it could be carried in a tipper, then Donald Malcolm would offer to carry it and it was a company rule that you didn't stop: 'Keep yourself busy,' was the one of the Man's favourite expressions.

Joining the garage staff in November 1954 was Hughie Hastie. And like many who came to Malcolms, he came to stay – for another 33 years

- while along the way he was promoted to foreman. Hughie had done his apprenticeship back in 1942 and after National Service was working down in South Ayrshire at a country garage when he heard that Malcolms were after a good mechanic: 'I wasn't making much money then,' recalls Hughie, 'so it was a good opportunity for me. Mrs Marion Malcolm actually tried her best to get my wife Nettie, my son Hugh and I a council house in Johnstone but when that couldn't be arranged, my wife stayed with her parents in Cumnock and I went into digs for a few months. Mrs Malcolm was to lend us £350 – interest free - so we could buy our own flat and we agreed that I paid it back at £10 per month. Mind at Christmas time and when it was holidays, Mrs Malcolm actually gave me the £10 payment back – and told me to spend it on the family. In total, she gave me back £60 and at that time, it was a lot of money - I'll never forget how good the Malcolms were to us.'

There was a huge improvement in Hughie's wage packet because while he had earned £6-10s a week in South Ayrshire, after his first week at Malcolms he took home £13: 'Mind I worked a lot of overtime,' he says, 'as for something like 20 years I must have worked 13 out of every 14 days. But give Donald his due, he always paid you for whatever overtime you worked.'

When Hughie joined Malcolms, Tommy Burns was the garage foreman while the other mechanics were Jimmy Wallace, Walter Bishop and Billy Kilpatrick. The garage staff normally clocked on at 8am but when they finished varied as to whether they were working 'wee' weeks or long ones. A long day saw you working until every job was finished (and that could be as late at 2am) as drivers had to record any vehicle defects on the 'Snag Sheet.' It's always been Malcolm's policy to ensure every vehicle possible is kept ready for the road and Hughie recalls even in those early days, they kept a huge supply of spares including engines, gearboxes and axles. While being the era before tilt cabs were in use, Malcolms made use of a large tree – just outside the garage – from which swung a block & tackle to make things like cab removal that much easier.

MACHRIHANISH

The work of the garage staff became more important once Malcolms took on a huge amount of work moving cement and ash in bulk. The construction of dams north of Glasgow saw the Malcolm drivers first grind their way over the awesome 'Rest and Be Thankful' climb, but then turn off the A83 after Cairndow for the long pull on a poorly made track to Allt na Lairige. The next dam built was near to Inverary at Glen Shira, but it was when the order was given for powder to build the Nato base airport at Machrihanish that the Malcolm drivers had to work really hard for their keep.

As the crow flies, Machrihanish is only about 50 miles or so southwest from Brookfield but being on the southern tip of The Mull of Kintyre (near Campbeltown) it's almost 150 road miles away. Doing one 300 mile round trip a day was hard going (never mind any more) although whenever possible, the Malcolm tippers would back load as there was a coalmine next to the airport.

A quartet of AEC Mercury four wheeled tippers (double sheeted to keep the load dry and with the back doors sealed tight with rags) were bought specifically for the cement runs and amongst their regular drivers were Willie Arthur, George Mason and Sandy Dixon. However, the biggest motor involved in this traffic was to be Malcolm's first artic – an S Type Bedford tipper. Sammy Stewart was its first driver, although it wasn't long before it was given to Bob Monoghan and the tales Bob can tell about his runs to Machrihanish can literally make your toes curl.

When the sun shines on the West coast of Scotland it can be a glorious place. On summer nights, the cement run was great and some drivers even took time out for a swim in one of the lochs. 'We used to have a sort of competition,' recalls Bob, 'as to who could travel the furthest – with the stick out – when we were running empty down the Rest and Be Thankful. It got a bit hairy but I reckon I could travel as far as the old torpedo factory on Loch Long which was a lot further than anyone else.'

Throwing the gear lever into neutral and coasting wasn't done in winter months as Bob reckoned he'd regularly need a double head (with an AEC on the chain pulling him up) for the climb: 'When we came down, I've seen me with an AEC on the front and one with a chain on the back as well just to stop me sliding off the road – things could be that bad on the Rest.'

MARRIAGE

Donald and Wilma were married on Saturday 23rd February 1957. Wilma recalls that it was snowing quite heavily at the time and her father – Andrew – had been concerned that the wedding taxis couldn't get through for the wedding party which included her sister Jessie as bridesmaid: 'Where we farmed at Uplawmoor was very exposed,' recalls Wilma. 'And while everyone made it to the wedding, I don't think everyone made it back home that night – things were that bad. But it didn't stop everyone enjoying themselves.'

Andrew Buchanan (Wilma's father) was a rather shy man and Wilma said he couldn't face the prospect of walking his daughter down the aisle of a large church with so many people looking on. Because of this, arrangements were made for the marriage to take place at the Grosvenor Hotel where Andrew gave Wilma away. There was to be something like 175 people at the Malcolm wedding (including Donald's best man Douglas Hamilton) although the newly married couple spent their first night together at another Glasgow hotel near Charring Cross.

The bad weather didn't prevent Donald &

Wilma heading south for England – and their whirlwind honeymoon. After the Sunday night at Scotch Corner Hotel, the Malcolms then went to relatives and friends at Preston and Blackpool – respectively – for a few nights, although Wilma recalls visiting a number of 'scrap yards' enroute before getting back home at Thursday lunch time: 'I know Donald bought at least one wagon somewhere on our travels – it may have been more,' she says.

Donald certainly bought one wagon because the following day, he was on the phone to Bert Brown: 'Here are the details, Bert, so get it covered on the insurance, get it taxed and find a driver for it because it's being delivered today and I want it out at work tomorrow.'

Donald was set to buy literally hundreds more wagons in the future because waiting in the wings were five men who were to have a big influence on the development of WH Malcolm. Although in truth, these five didn't yet realise how big an influence Donald Malcolm was to have on them.

Donald and Wilma were married at the Grosvenor Hotel in Glasgow on 23rd February 1957. Sharing the group photograph (opposite) are Marion Malcolm – sat on the right – and Wilma's mother, also called Wilma, being sat on the left. Sharing the back row with the bride & groom are – from the right – Wilma's father Andrew; the best man Douglas Hamilton; Wilma's sister Jessie and Bob Malcolm. Bob was an uncle of Donald being his father Walter's youngest brother.

CHAPTER 4

The Grampian Five

In the 21st century they would probably be called Venture Capitalists but back in 1958, the five original founders of Grampian Holdings Ltd thought it was just good business sense to pool their efforts in acquiring solid business concerns, which would thrive through better financial backing and management support. The founding five were Colonel David Greig, Sir James Hutchinson, Jock Mackenzie, Neil Morris and Commander John Alexander Paul. All were well known in their own right and even now, Morris Furniture is still a well-known name on the Glasgow business scene.

The five's first acquisition was a defunct concern called The Bowanlea Tea Estates Ltd. This was first incorporated as a limited company on 10th August 1921 but in 1958 was part of Minister Trust Ltd and was simply a shell concern. However, to emphasise the 'Scottishness' of the new business venture, the name of the Bowanlea company was changed to Grampian Holdings Ltd on 22nd April 1958.

With the preliminaries out of the way, Grampian was to make their first acquisition in early 1959 when they bought Lanarkshire Bolt (Holdings) Ltd. As a reflection of the diversity of their interests, other 1959 Grampian acquisitions included a structural steel fabrication company, a London furniture manufacturer, an Oban based Harris Tweed manufacturer and a group of Wembley based concerns involved in the importation and manufacture of light fittings.

TEA AND SCONES

As Grampian were slowly establishing their credibility on the Stock Exchange, the main concern of Marion Malcolm – who was then aged 69 - was what would happen when she died. The 1959 profits (before taxation) of the Malcolm concern were £54,775 and as she was in joint partnership with her son Donald, she realised that as and when death duties were collected, it would have a huge impact on the Malcolm business viability. Marion would have another 15 years or so of her life to lead but it indicates her astuteness in not wanting to give away what the family had strived so hard to build together.

According to the 1960 records of Grampian Holdings, Donald had been made partner – with his mother – in 1939 when still aged 14. Marion could of course have just passed her share of Walter H Malcolm to her son but both mother & son felt this was the time to get extra muscle into their business.

The first move was to create WH Malcolm Ltd which in turn acquired the business of the Walter H Malcolm partnership and some (but not all) of its assets. The next step was to seek out someone who would buy up this family owned Limited business but as a going concern and not just for the assets.

In 1960, many family owned companies were in a similar position to the Malcolms and there were several options available to them. The Transport Development Group were steadily buying road haulage concerns throughout the UK as was the United Transport Group. While even the NFC (British Road Services) was expanding again through buying up successful haulage concerns.

The 1950s had been a good time for the WH Malcolm business. Although it made a loss (of £3,586) during 1951, a steady growth in both fleet size and profits meant the late 1960 figures were a fleet size of 37 vehicles (and 10 mechanical shovels) and a previous year profit figure of £68,010 – before taxation.

This obvious growth – and success – during the decade meant several approaches (regarding a take over) were made to them. These weren't acted upon, but after an approach by the newly formed Grampian Holdings, an invitation was given to the Grampian management to come and enjoy tea & scones at Brookfield.

It's always very difficult to value any concern. True, you can calculate asset worth through accounts and other reference books but when it comes to the variable of 'Good Will' then its value can be anyone's guess. And how do you put a price on the prospect of having the vibrant 35-year-old Donald Malcolm at the company helm? Neil Morris was amongst the Grampian deputation who went to see mother & son and he later recalled the meeting as being very different to the norm: 'Mrs Wilma Malcolm had baked some very nice scones,' he said, 'but every time we were offered another one, the value of the WH Malcolm business seemed to go up by another £1,000. They were very expensive scones which we enjoyed.'

The final agreed price of the transaction was £216,000, which was made up of £189,000 in cash and the balance of 23,685 Ordinary Shares of 5 shillings each of Grampian.

Both sides of the agreement were to benefit in the long term from their joint venture. Donald Malcolm and WH Malcolm Ltd were given the financial support they needed while Grampian Holdings Ltd acquired their first asset in what would be their massive Road Transport and Haulage Division.

As part of the sale, Donald agreed to stay on for 10 years as Chairman and Managing Director of WH Malcolm Ltd but as time was to tell, he stayed on for the rest of his life. Also joining the Board of WH Malcolm Ltd in November 1960 as directors were Jack Love (who was also still a director with the Lind quarry concern) and Mr J Cole-Hamilton, a partner in a firm of Glasgow based chartered accountants.

Although then becoming an employee – albeit as Chairman – Donald was always very guarded in how he spent (Grampian's) money. 'Donald Malcolm was never extravagant,' recalls Bill Hughes who later spent 21 years as Chief Executive / Chairman of Grampian plc. 'He always understood he was part of a large Group and realised that he had to earn dividends for his shareholders and in truth, he managed the company's money as though it was his own – he was always very careful.'

Although owning several thousand of Grampian shares, Donald was never a financial wheeler-dealer: 'In all the time I knew him,' says Bill, 'I don't think he ever bought or sold any of those original shares. His financial heart was very much old school and he was far happier knowing his money was safely ensconced in the bank.' Or, as explained later, being invested back into lorries and even property.

SIXTIES SURGE

It's probably at this point in the Malcolm story that we should pause and reflect. From the moment when Donald and Marion Malcolm signed the paperwork in November 1960 relinquishing ownership of WH Malcolm Ltd to Grampian, it was the end of an era. Things had changed a lot in the business, which Marion Malcolm had nurtured from those traumatic days back in 1934. However, her input into Donald's thoughts was always respected and in agreeing to stay on as a Director of the new company, she would contribute over 10 years of wisdom into how the Company developed.

Marion had become a grandmother when Donald & Wilma's first child (also christened Wilma) was born in 1958 and from then on, the term of 'Granny Malcolm' was used to refer to her by family, friends, staff and even other residents of Brookfield. This was purely a term of endearment, as Marion was generally very well liked by all who knew and met her. She had a more placid nature (when compared to her son, Donald) although it's said that if she ever slipped into Gaelic – under her breath – then you knew she was getting exasperated.

It was also a big day of change for Donald as no longer was he owner of his own domain and it was now members of the board – and Grampian shareholders – who could ask him questions. That may have been the theory although in practice, Donald gave little thought to the transition. In fact he needed little time to settle into his new roll as things were set to surge through the '60s. And if anything, Donald Malcolm put even more effort into continuing the success of his growing concern.

There are only about four years between these two views of the Malcolm fleet line up pictured in the Boghouse yard (see also next page). But the big differences from 1957 and 1961 are shown in the far better loading shovels, far newer TJ Bedford four wheelers plus brand new fuel tanks and yard surface. Plus, a brand new Rover car for the boss. Seen at the right rear of shot (above) is the quartet of

AEC Mercury four-wheel tippers, which includes OHS 667. Their sheeted bodies indicating their use on the fly ash traffic, a job also done by the company's first artic, the S type Bedford, seen to their left. Although Bedfords still took the lion share of the Malcolm fleet – in 1961 – the presence of seven Thames Traders suggested the scales of Malcolm preference was heading towards Ford.

Saturday afternoon in the 1950s never saw many Malcolm drivers in the yard. But those of the garage staff who were present (and can be identified) when the fleet shot of 1957 photograph was taken on pages 36 and 37 are – right to left: Peter Muldoon; Duncan McCormack; Bert Brown – in the jumper – Hughie Clarke; Willie Smith; the smartly attired Hughie Hastie (in the suit) with his wife Nettie and young son Hugh; Fulton Love; Derek McGregor; Jackie Aitkin; Joe McManus and Angus Macfadzean. LHS 70 was the Austin A35 allocated to Bert Brown.

WHS 933 was new to Malcolms in 1963 and one of only two Commer two-stroke artics ran at that time. Seen with a load of main steam pipes (from Babcock) on the York semi-trailer, Malcolm's also used it with a Taskers Little Giant low loader. Not the best liked vehicles in the fleet at the time – although they were probably the noisiest – Robert McFarlane and Fulton Love are recalled as being this vehicle's regular drivers.

CHAPTER 5

Widening Horizons

It took less than a month for Donald to convince the Grampian Board to make their next transport acquisition. William Wilson & Son (Johnstone) Ltd was formed to acquire the business and some of the assets of William Wilson & Son – which was then owned by Martin Wilson. Because it was very similar in nature, it dovetailed easily into the WH Malcolm Ltd activities and saw the Grampian transport fleet expand with 17 more vehicles and five more earth-moving machines.

The next purchase was Wilson Brothers (Haulage) Ltd, which came into the Grampian fold in December 1961. It was to be the structure and assets of this company, which was to give the WH Malcolm the platform for widening their horizons. And once Donald Malcolm had put his mind to it, the horizon was as wide as he could want it.

Up until the early 1960s, the Malcolm business had always been very localised. With most of the tipper fleet only having 'B' licences, it meant the type of traffic – and the distance they would travel – was tightly controlled by the Carriers Licence legislation then in force. However, once the fleet of Wilson Brothers (Haulage) Ltd was bought, the whole make up of Malcolms was set to change in both the nature of its traffic and where the vehicles could operate to.

The long established Wilson Brothers concern then had Mathew Wilson in control and was based in Canal Street at Johnstone. The company's speciality had grown from the traditional 'Carrier' system where smalls were delivered to all parts of the surrounding area – after collections had been made in and around Glasgow. The Wilson Brothers fleet was then about 15 strong (and painted yellow, brown & red) but perhaps of more significant interest was the fact that all these vehicles were equipped with 'A' licences. The Wilson customer base was extensive and featured a number of blue chip concerns as generally speaking the 'A' licences allowed the vehicles to carry anything – and go

anywhere. And while Donald Malcolm had no experience of long distance general haulage work, he knew these licences – and the Wilson Brothers portfolio of contacts - was the key to developing a major part of the Malcolm business.

MOVE TO BROOKFIELD

More than 40 years on, it's hard to fully appreciate the significance of taking on – and extending – the Wilson Brothers operation. Donald Malcolm recalled that at that time, considering any delivery work which took his vehicles south of Hamilton (on the south eastern suburbs of Glasgow) was done with some trepidation. If you snapped Donald Malcolm in half, you would discover he was a tipper man, through and through. However, as we all know, Donald never flinched from doing what his gut feeling told him was right, so he soon re-organised the whole work pattern of the old Wilson Brothers fleet. First of all, some of the vehicles were moved from Canal Street to Brookfield and then instead of just delivering around the doors, the ex Wilson Brothers driver's instructions then generally saw them head for anywhere in the UK.

Amongst those who made the move to Brookfield were Robert English and Frank Murney. It wasn't Frank's first experience of working for the Malcolm family as his father - James – was one of the Malcolm family's earliest drivers. And of course, whenever he wasn't at school, young Frank would often ride with his father and even help out when shovelling was required: 'I remember Donald giving me a size 6 shovel and saying that when I grew up, he would give me something bigger – but in truth, I never really grew much taller. At the end of the day, Granny Malcolm always asked if Donald had paid me for helping out and she'd normally give me a buttie as well – she was great.'

When he did leave school, Francis – as Granny

Malcolm always called him – started out as a van boy with Wilson Brothers and Robert English actually taught him how to drive. Both Robert and Frank were to remain with WH Malcolm Ltd for the rest of their working lives, which tells you they weren't too fazed about their new working itinerary – or their new boss: 'Donald was a hard taskmaster,' recalls Robert, 'and if you were a slacker, it was perhaps best if you just said good bye to start with – because Donald would soon be after you. He had a good choice of vocabulary but it was always best to admit to things – even if you'd done wrong – and feel the wrath of his tongue, because if you told lies, he'd always find you out. I thought he was a great boss to work for – he was a one off.'

The Wilson fleet had long favoured Bedfords so the first taste of long distance work - for Robert and Frank – was with their TK Bedford artics, which had Scammell single axle trailers. Most of their outward-bound traffic was sourced from Babcock & Wilcox who were building a huge number of power stations across the UK. While Malcolms didn't handle the abnormal

Babcock traffic (folk like Pickfords and McKelvies did their heavy haulage) it was the lighter, specialised type of awkward wide pipe work that filled their semi-trailers.

As the Babcock work took off, the TKs were first replaced with stronger AEC Mercury tractor units – and then even stronger AEC Mandators. Robert then recalls an early ERF – JHS 257D – before taking delivery of LHS 354E, his first Volvo F86. Although most vivid memories are with some of the first Scania Vabis tractor units which came into Scotland.

All these long distance tractor units were fitted with day cabs and while some drivers of the era often slept – in the cab – over the bonnet, favourite digs for both Robert and Frank was Ma Shipers at Penrith: 'She charged 10 shillings (50p) for dinner, bed and breakfast but I reckon it was the best digs in the country,' said Robert. 'She had beds in a couple of houses and while there was always a late night supper left out, the early starters could even cook their own breakfasts if they wanted to.'

Journey times for the long distance outfits

These superb aerial photographs show the new Murray Street depot in Paisley shortly after Malcolms moved their tipper fleet out of Brookfield in September 1964. With Donald taking his main office here, it became the company's administrative HQ – and Donald's second home. The premises adjacent are Irvine Caravans although in the late 1970s, this land would also be bought and utilised as vehicle hard standing as the Malcolm tipper numbers grew. LAD Dodges and Ford Thames Traders seem to make up the bulk of the Malcolm tipper vehicles pictured in residence.

were a lot longer in those pre-motorway days of the 1960s as the likes of Beattock – in Scotland – and the A6 over Shap could be a nightmare in the bad weather. However, Robert recalls his longest trip was when he headed north for Dounreay: 'It was a lovely day here,' recalled Robert, 'but when I got to Helmsdale, the police stopped me because the A9 was blocked with snow. After a couple of days, I eventually got to Thurso but it took another five days before the road to the power station was opened up for goods vehicles. And of course, just to make things worse, when I was coming back, I got a puncture at Inverness and couldn't get a new tyre until the following day, so that was another night out.'

EXPERTISE

The problem with doing long distance work has always been the concern of empty running on the return. With so much competition (even in 'A' licence days) getting suitable back loads was the key to operational efficiency. Malcolm drivers themselves often had to ring round Clearing Houses to find something suitable and Robert English recalls that Inverdon Transport in London was a good source of Scottish bound traffic. However, such an informal structure was very hit & miss, so to enhance the general haulage side of Malcolms, Donald advertised for traffic managers – specifically with general haulage expertise in mind. Amongst those who answered the various ads – and who were to become part of the Malcolm team for many years – were John Melrose and Tom Hamilton.

John had spent 14 years working for the Edinburgh based Sadler Transport and was immediately pitched in to manage the newly acquired Tyne Street, Glasgow (Haulage) Ltd. This limited company had been formed to acquire the vehicles and property of John McDonald (Haulage) Ltd with 26 vehicles being operated on the day of acquisition in January 1965.

Prior to the purchase, Peter McDonald had been running the company and four of his nephews – James, Alistair, Charles & Colin, had been involved. The vehicles however were virtually scrap and all were immediately replaced with 10 Dodge four-wheel flats, six assorted Foden / AEC artics and three, six wheel rigids recalled as amongst the new vehicles going into service.

This Tyne Street depot soon had extra vehicles added as the 17-vehicle strong haulage business of Collingwood Engineering Co. Ltd was acquired. This had been part of John Lawrence Builders Ltd and John was well known in Glasgow at that time as being the owner of Rangers football club.

William Wilson & Son had been a competitor of Walter Malcolm when he first started his coal round in 1925. So it was rather poignant when this Wilson business was brought into the Grampian / WH Malcolm fold in December 1960. Although painted in corporate Malcolm colours, the William Wilson name (and base at Russell Street, Johnstone) was retained until about 1995. Loading the Ford 'D' Series tipper (with Tommy Ross believed behind the wheel) is long serving shovel driver Willie Anderson – he did 36 years with Malcolms from 1961. Willie recalls the Cat 966B as being a good old tool of the period. Capable of lifting some 4 tons in the bucket, Willie thinks the photograph was either taken at Twechar Bing, Kirkintilloch or Cambuslang. Willie recalls later working for 10 years at East Calder loading the trains which Malcolms used to haul blaes to the Pacific Quay terminal in Glasgow – prior to onward distribution.

The Albion Reiver proved a long serving workhorse for Malcolms and although SHS 44G is designated a Super Reiver, tipper driver Jim McGlynn recalls how they could fry you in the summer yet freeze you in the winter. Most famous of all the Malcolm Reivers must be the one Mark Penman drove. Employed by John McDonald, when that company was taken over in 1965, he was driving a CX Albion four wheeler and trailer GGG 395. 'Overnight we all got brand new vehicles – Reivers, Dodges and Thames Traders. But my new Reiver was up-rated to pull a new Dyson trailer – or an independent dolly, for long loads. I think mine was the only one in the Malcolm Group which did that.' Mark – and his trailer mate James McGorm – did all sorts of loads with their Reiver. And while it doesn't come with a trailer, the model maker Corgi's re-creation of a WH Malcolm Reiver comes with Mark's old registration – CHS 487C.

Surrounded by houses, Tyne Street was not the best place for a haulage depot but being located in Central Glasgow was very handy for serving Glasgow customers – and for attracting drivers. John Melrose well recalls the intensity of the operation: 'My working day normally started at 6am and as Donald normally rang about 7.30am to see how things were going, I knew I had to have everyone out before then. At times, that meant knocking on the doors of drivers homes just to get them up.'

Tyne Street had a huge variety of traffic – and also a big customer base, which pleased Donald: 'If we had 40 wagons,' said John, 'it was Donald's ideal that we had 40 different customers for them. So if one customer went quiet – or even went broke – it meant we only had to find work for one vehicle.'

John Melrose is still on the Malcolm staff and he still misses The Big Man: 'Donald was an amazing man,' he said. 'I still miss his great enthusiasm for the job – and his memory. He didn't like people who weren't committed to the job but if you worked hard for him – and ever got into bother - he'd help you out 100 per cent. Those who knew Donald will tell you he had a heart of gold.'

The pressure on space was eased for Tyne Street staff once Grampian Holdings moved their HQ to a plot of land they bought in Castlebank Street, Glasgow around 1973. After building Stag House, there was more than enough space left on this ex Clyde Port Authority land to build a depot for Malcolms. The operation saw a mix of flats and tippers based here and while John Melrose's staff had to look after the flat traffic, all the tippers were controlled through the Murray Street (Paisley) depot.

TRANSPORT ASOCIATION

Although Brookfield will always be the ancestral heart of Malcolms, in July 1964 the administrative centre of affairs – as well as the company's tipper operation - were moved to a purpose built site in Murray Street, Paisley. The reason behind the move was simply the huge expansion which had taken place – in such a very short time. When Malcolms were bought by Grampian in 1960, the road going fleet was counted at 37 strong but 10 years later, 332 vehicles were being operated within the Group.

With all the tippers gone, it didn't mean things were quiet at Brookfield – far from it. There will be more on Malcolm's Plant operation later, but given the brief to sort out the general haulage side of Malcolms at Brookfield was to be Tom Hamilton. Tom had learnt his craft first as a driver and then as a Traffic Controller (on the Massey Ferguson contract) with the large Kilmarnock haulier of McKinnons.

However, when that concern was absorbed into the Tayforth Group in September 1965, Tom reckoned it was time to look elsewhere: 'Malcolms were advertising for a general haulage traffic man but I didn't think much of it at first because I always thought Malcolms were just tipper people.'

Tom actually went for three interviews with the last one being when Donald's mother, Marion, gave him the nod: 'Donald later told me he knew I was the man for the job as soon as he saw me,' said Tom, 'because I reminded him very much of his father.'

In 1965, the Brookfield general haulage operation involved 24 flat wagons, with half that number being four wheelers – Dodge, Albion and Bedford. A lot of the work – at that time - was either dedicated contract hire or time work. But as soon as Tom found his feet, he realised how quickly things could change: 'At Tayforth, it took an eternity to get anything changed, but once Donald realised what you were after, a decision quickly came.'

An early decision to join the long established Transport Association proved to be a good one. This informal mix of general hauliers – spread across the country – proved an ideal chain of depots both to draw fuel and supply back loads: 'We soon began using DM Smith (of Wishaw) for back loads out of London and Welch's of Stapleford were another good TA contact.' However, the key to the subsequent huge expansion of the Malcolm general haulage operation was already within their own portfolio.

Amongst the many customers inherited with the Wilson Brothers operation had been the food manufacturer of Heinz. Originally this had seen the Malcolm (Wilson) vehicles undertake shop deliveries from the Paisley factory, but when Malcolms were asked if they could undertake some long distance work from the Heinz Kit Green factory at Wigan, Tom Hamilton jumped at it: 'Our first place down there was some rented premises at Newton-le-Willows,' said Tom, 'and the ex Allison Transport man Bob Hay ran it. I think originally we were asked to move four loads a day but things soon snowballed, so very soon we moved to a bigger place at Lostock Hall, Preston.'

The Heinz work lasted for about 10 years and allowed Malcolms to establish both their North West England credentials and the ability to run over night trunk services back into Scotland.

As well as Brookfield, general haulage trunk

motors were ran into Malcolm's Kilwinning depot. In 1967, William Kerr (Kilwinning) Ltd had been bought by Grampian and the Kerr fleet then had been 26 strong – albeit again in questionable condition and in need of immediate updating. Jimmy Paterson was given the brief to sort out the ex Kerr operation which at the time was based right in the centre of town at Woodwynd (off Hamilton Street). Although only 20 or so miles south east of Paisley, Kilwinning was an ideal entry point to the customer base of Ayrshire and it also helped the Malcolm cause that the Kerr operation had been a 50/50 mix of tippers and flats.

The flat traffic from here was to be as diverse as you could imagine. Tom Hamilton had just won some good steel work through Colvilles of Glengarnoch in Ayrshire, but the Kerr contacts saw Malcolms carrying Rockware glass, specialist fuel and oils from Shell at Ardrossan as well as explosives from ICI. The Rockware traffic in particular proved to be the best long-term contact,

for as well as sourcing outward bound loads from Ayrshire, the Rockware plants in Yorkshire were an ideal source of back loads to Scotland.

This suited Malcolms very well, especially when Babcock were involved in the construction of Drax Power Station near Selby. All manner of awkward fabrications were carried south on long length trailers, which proved to be an odd sight, when subsequently back loaded with new glass whiskey bottles out of Castleford. Not that this practice was illegal, it's just the Yorkshire folk weren't used to the dynamics of Malcolms.

The quick decision making of Donald saw him give Tom Hamilton a directorship – within two years of him joining the company. While within another couple of years (1969) it was realised the general haulage fleet had outgrown their Brookfield base so premises on Gas Street in Johnstone – Cartside – were acquired and another slice of the Malcolm Empire made its exodus from Brookfield, although still very much under control of the Big Man.

New to WH Malcolm in 1963, this 9.6 litre powered AEC Mandator did all sorts of work but it didn't deliver these two 3 ton fermentation tanks – well not on this trailer. Bob Monoghan recalls how it took a day – during March 1965 - to get them loaded in the Paisley premises of Miller Brothers. But when he tried to get out of the works gate, he realised the running height of over 16'6" was too high for things like power cables, low bridges and even tram wires. 'We spent the next day taking them off and I took them up – one at a time – to Dallas North near Elgin using a low loader trailer. But of course Donald got a back load for me from Ullapool.' Bob's mate for that job – and many other wide loads – was Jimmy McGorm: 'He was a brilliant second man and under his guidance, he could put you anywhere,' said Bob. Thanks to the good observation of Robert Deans, this AEC was found fully restored (by Alan Sime) in Dundee. It's since been re-bought by the company and is now repainted into its original WH Malcolm colours.

Talk to any of the WH Malcolm artic drivers of the late 1960s and you'll probably see their eyes mist over, as they wax lyrical over the attributes of their first Scania-Vabis tractor units. Bob Monoghan recalls taking one out for a test run and then getting a call on the two way radio: 'The police had complained about me blasting through Glasgow and they wanted the company to tell me to slow down.' Frank Murney has fond memories of out-dragging Minis away from traffic lights so all in all, these first Scanias were like a breath of fresh air. One vehicle, which didn't live up to its name, was XHS 405H – their first Scania 80 Super. 'I think it was the worst vehicle Donald ever bought,' said Robert English, who speaks from his lengthy company experience. 'It was far too light and just generally under-powered – it was just awful.' The drivers pictured below are – from left to right – Martin McFee, Robert English, Gordon McDonald and Bobby Murie. Gordon McDonald normally drove an ERF at that time and only stood in the line to make up the quartet as Tony Carruthers normally drove this vehicle.

With Donald being such good friends with Jim McKelvie, it wasn't surprising that when Jim set up Ailsa Trucks – as importers of Volvos – then Malcolms would certainly try their offerings. And the fact that they soon found the product so good is reflected in this line up seen at the Cartside yard in 1970. Taking pole position – at the front – is YHS 651H, the usual vehicle of driver Gordon McDonald. However,

perhaps more noteworthy is the brace of N series – bonneted – Volvos at the back. Malcolms had four in total – two, four wheelers and two six wheelers – and when they arrived from Sweden, they were the first company vehicles to have tachographs fitted.

The Malcolm family – very much at ease – seen at the WH Malcolm staff dance around 1977. Walter is on the left, stood next to Wilma, Marion and Andrew.

CHAPTER 6

Family Affairs

If you signed up to work for Donald Malcolm, then you were expected to give full value for your wage packet. Yes, this has been said before but it's a point that must be emphasised – the Big Man expected nothing else. Perhaps the reason he demanded 100% from everyone was he gave exactly the same – if not more.

Donald's day generally started about 5am – when he got out of bed. The rest of the house may have been fast asleep so Donald's breakfast - at that early hour – may have only been a King Edward cigar. Getting out to see that his men were out was his main priority and all the staff – be it management, drivers or mechanics – knew Donald could appear at any time, day or night, at any of the Malcolm depots or operations. In fact his huge distinctive presence was more than likely to appear if you were doing something you shouldn't have been doing.

For refreshment, Donald preferred to drink a mug of tea – with milk and sugar - rather than coffee and he'd normally built up an appetite before he'd head back to Boghouse for his cooked breakfast after 9am. He'd squeeze in time then for a wet shave ('He had about three electric razors,' recalled Wilma, 'but he said they'd never give him a proper shave') but breakfast - and lunch - were always taken at full speed. In fact, Wilma recalls Mrs Murphy – who helped her around the house – being upset at the way Donald ate so quickly: 'It's a pity he's only allowed 20 minutes for his lunch,' Mrs Murphy used to say. The Big Man could have taken as long as he wanted but Donald reckoned anything longer was just a waste. True in later years, he took time out for a 20-30 minutes sleep in the chair – after lunch – but then it was back into the car and off on his calls.

The next time Wilma might see Donald was generally after 8pm: 'He hardly ever saw the kids during the week,' she says, 'although he'd always call and see his mother on the way home.' As many people can testify, Donald loved to eat – although only certain food: 'He liked his food fairly plain,' said Wilma. 'Soup, mince & tatties, steak and perhaps apple cake & custard.' Not a big spicy food lover (he'd never touch Chinese or Indian food) even haggis was only eaten on the special occasion of Burns Supper although, in later years, he loved the other Scottish staple of porridge.

Donald was brought up to always clean his plate – before leaving the table – and Wilma laughs that he'd also clear the kids plates as well so it's perhaps no surprise that Big Donald's weight was to creep over 21 stones. However, for such a big man, Donald was particularly agile and light on his feet (no wonder he loved dancing so much) although if he ever shook your hand, you realised how massive his palms were.

As well as his premature grey hair (and the distinctive aroma of Kuduos after shave) another Donald Malcolm trademark was his trouser bracers, although if he did go out on a night, he'd change these for a dress pair. With having so many friends, Donald & Wilma received all manner of social invitations but they'd never go out and leave Boghouse unattended. True it was more secure if someone was always on the premises, but Donald's main concern was ensuring the phone would always be answered. He never wanted a customer to complain they could never speak to anyone at Malcolms.

Although Donald may have looked – and sounded – as the typical road haulier, one aspect of the stereotype in which he was totally different was how he was almost tee total: 'He liked to drive whenever we went out,' said Wilma, 'so he never drank. On a special occasion I've seen him pressed into having half a glass of red wine although back at home – and last thing at night – he did like a drop of brandy & ginger before going to bed.'

Not a big TV lover (apart from motoring programmes and things like 'Taggart') Donald would simply speed read the newspapers which came to Boghouse – The Daily Express, The Glasgow Herald and The Daily Record. He did however read – from cover to cover – the weekly publications Commercial Motor and Motor Transport. His other regular night time reading was the individual tipper vehicles' daily earning sheets – just to make sure everyone else was working as hard as possible and doing their maximum number of loads.

Donald's day would end long after 12 midnight although last phone call of the day – or night – was normally to good mate Jimmy Yuill. And of course, his next working day would of course start again at 5am. Weekends were slightly different in that Donald could be home on a Saturday afternoon by 2.30pm. While Sunday was often spent visiting drivers at home who were on long term sick (or updating his infamous little black book) but it was almost guaranteed that 6pm on a Sunday was the time for the Sunday roast with the family.

HOLIDAYS

When you kept up such a hectic pace as Donald Malcolm, you'd anticipate that he would really look forward to his fortnight 'Glasgow Fair' holiday in mid July, but – in truth – holidays and Donald Malcolm just didn't mix. Whenever the family went to either the Bruce Hotel at Carnoustie or the Imperial Hotel at Blackpool, it was a chance to catch up with friends and relations in the area but generally speaking, Donald spent most of his early holidays inside the nearest public phone box. And when he had a room with a phone in it – in a far off land - often's the case that the subsequent bill for meals & accommodation on the holiday was actually exceeded by the bill for phone calls – such was the Big Man's use of this lifeline back to Scotland. Although not a big lover of foreign holidays, Donald did travel as far as Monte Carlo, Switzerland, Tenerife and Jersey but Wilma – and the rest of the family – soon realised even when he was away, his thoughts were very much back in Renfrewshire.

Donald and Wilma are seen almost in the centre of a group of some very good friends. The other five couples are (not necessarily stood together): John and Janet Young; Willie and May Martin; Martin and Mary Wilson; George and Sadie Cunningham plus Jim and Marion Muir.

Donald and Wilma are seen enjoying another night out. 'I'll never forget – as a kid – noticing how my Dad used two hair brushes – and cream - to smooth down his hair before he went out,' recalls his son Andrew.

Donald & Wilma were to have four children. Their first-born – Wilma - was followed by another daughter Marion and then the two sons Walter and Andrew. To the two boys – especially – the Malcolm yard was a great place to live and play in, even though both the general haulage and plant side of the business had offices in two different parts of Boghouse.

Mixing with the staff was routine for the children although Walter Malcolm recalls two people in particular from those early days: 'Aubrey Gundry was a Cornishman by birth but he came to us – as an outside supervisor – straight from the Marines. I remember he didn't have much hair and when we'd shout "Hey Baldy" he'd chase after us with his stick. But he took it in good fun.'

Dick Barnes was another distinctive Brookfield character: 'He had a shock of red hair and a red face but because he spray painted all the motors, his hair tended to change colour depending on what colour paint he'd been spraying. He lived in Johnstone but he often just fell asleep in the boiler room,' recalled Walter.

The Malcolm family were brought up amongst the thriving activity of Brookfield but without any concession to their surroundings or status. 'We just treat the Malcolms as normal people,' recalled the late long serving Malcolm tipper driver William Ballantyne. 'Yes, they may have had more money than us but it was always first name terms with everyone. And in the early days of his marriage, I've even seen Donald bring us all a present when he came back from holiday – new size 12 shovels!!'

While all the drivers seemed to enjoy chauffeuring Granny Malcolm into Glasgow for something special, even Donald's sisters seemed to mix in well: 'I can remember Agnes often stopping at the bus stop on a night and asking if we wanted a lift back into Johnstone,' says William. 'She wasn't at all bothered that we were all wearing dirty overalls.'

Willie was amongst the tipper driver exodus that made the move to Murray Street in 1964 although – before he left – he was to have a big influence on Andrew Malcolm at the tender age of 2. 'I suppose I gave him his first driving lesson,' said Willie. 'We had this small tractor at Brookfield which was kitted out with sweeping brushes to keep the yard clean. I lifted Andrew up on to it one day, set the hand throttle and put it into gear and he was immediately in his element as he drove it round the yard.'

The impression that – and other tasting experiences – made with the youngest Malcolm was destined to have a major effect on the entire Malcolm organisation. But as Andrew was entering his teens, the linch-pin of the Malcolm family was saying her last good bye.

GRANNY MALCOLM BOWS OUT

Historically, transport has generally been a male dominated industry and while Donald Malcolm was the driving force behind the company's growth & success, he'd be the first to endorse the huge influence, which Marion Malcolm had on affairs. Even now – more than 30 years after her death – if you speak to anyone who knew her, you'll only hear complimentary remarks about her.

While Donald may have sworn like a trooper (although never in front of the young children at home) Granny Malcolm needed just her presence and perhaps a certain look to demonstrate her thoughts. She never forgot her roots – in the Western Isles – and was to donate a lot of money to the Church back there. And even in her final days, she was thinking of others, more than herself: 'I don't want to be a burden on anyone,' she said about the prospect of ill health approaching.

She must have had a premonition of what was to happen, because when Donald went to pick her up to go into hospital, she asked to be driven back round via the Boghouse depot: 'It might be the last time I see the place,' she explained. She was right because within a month, she had died of bowel cancer.

Even though she was 84, it was a huge loss for Donald and the entire Malcolm family. There were more than 100 wreaths sent from well-wishers and because of the huge numbers who wanted to be present, the funeral service was held in the converted barn (which had also seen service as the traffic office) at Boghouse. Marion was to be buried at Houston cemetery and while her passing left a huge gap, it didn't stop Donald on his onward crusade.

Donald is seen with his mother Marion and his wife Wilma. The stance – with his hands lightly clasped in front of him – is well recognised by his son Andrew who admits that both he and his brother Walter have a similar way of standing. 'The only thing missing in that photograph with my Dad is seeing him with his car keys in his fingers – he always seemed to stand like that.'

Donald was always very close to his mother Marion and stopping off to see her at her house 'Shawbost' was at least a daily occurrence. When Donald was later asked about modern-day man management training and techniques, he always said he tended to work on his gut instinct – and did what came naturally. While that approach always seemed to stand Donald in good stead, he said he'd learnt the technique from his mother, whom he reckoned was gifted with a second sight.

Due to their large circle of friends, Donald and Wilma were invited to numerous weddings. And even though Donald's preferred mode of dress for a weekend was a comfortable cardigan – with holes in the elbows – he of course always dressed up smartly for the occasion. However, Wilma always breathed a sigh of relief, if they got to the church without encountering a broken down Malcolm vehicle, or any other excuse for Donald to crawl under something and put right.

The 30 strong fleet of Dunfermline based John Hutchison was bought in 1964 and although the vehicles painted in the corporate Grampian / Malcolm livery, the new arrangement never seemed to blend with the rest of the Grampian transport arm. So in 1972, this business was sold back to the Hutchison family.

In the late 1960s, Ford announced they were ceasing manufacture of the bonneted 'K' Series model. But as Donald felt the model was such a good workhorse, he persuaded Ford to make 100 more of them, which Malcolms and another Glasgow haulier – Robert Pollock – would share. Brought north by train – in chassis cab form – they were bodied by Edbro and spread round the Group. EHS 117J was allocated to Kilwinning and regular driver Willie Townsley. Gordon Lauder recalls the one he had because the steering was so heavy, it would pull your arms off. George Scott recalls how awkward it was to remove the gearbox prior to replacing the clutch: 'It took three of us – and a lump of rope to do that job.' Best turned out 'K' must have been the Russell Street based George Addison: 'He did council work and his motor was so clean, you could eat your dinner off it,' said George.

Kilwinning vehicles may have looked identical to the rest of the Malcolm operation but the type of traffic generated by this Ayrshire depot could vary in the extreme. This Leyland Bison was regularly used for explosives traffic, which took driver – and his extra attendant – all over the country. While the work may have sounded daunting, to young Andrew McLune, it was a way of earning extra money. Andrew is the son of Kilwinning's Dave McLune - foreman mechanic at the time – and he was looking to earn the cash to see him through his studies. 'You had to be prepared to work as an attendant at a moments notice,' said Andrew, 'as it wasn't known when the job had to be done. But I enjoyed the trips – and there were never any problems.'

CHAPTER 7

What's in a Name

You don't need to study the Malcolm history for very long to realise it is complicated. With the huge number of companies taken over by Grampian – during the expansive '60s – it's not surprising there were all manner of different concerns and trading names seen on Malcolm premises. While some of these companies were bought for the vital Carriers licences, they all came with their own customer base. JL McNeil Ltd of Renfrew was one such concern that was acquired in August 1964 and this purchase saw 14 vehicles (mainly tippers) brought into the Group operation. There were 21 vehicles added to the Malcolm Group fleet list when John Johnstone (Contractors) Ltd was acquired in January 1967. Originally based in Baltic Lane, premises in Westerburn Street, Glasgow was soon found for this operation, which Bobby Summers originally managed. Goodwill towards these long established businesses was one of the main reasons, why these names were retained long after the vehicles may have been painted into the corporate Malcolm blue colours.

Generally speaking, each concern gave a boost to the Malcolm / Grampian business although one exception which didn't fully work out was that of John Hutchison & Son (Haulage) Ltd. When it was bought in July 1964, the company was operating 30 vehicles and two earth-moving machines. However with Hutchisons being based in Fife, it was found that their operation didn't gel with the rest of the Grampian work. So, on 1st January 1972, the company was sold back to John Hutchison, who with his father – Jack – had owned the business originally.

LOANHEAD TRANSPORT

Although the Hutchison business had been owned by Grampian, one company that was never part of the corporate owner (until its vehicles were bought in February 2001) was Loanhead Transport Ltd. Back in 1967, Donald Malcolm and Bill Lind had joined forces and invested – as a joint venture – in the new company and bought four new TK Bedford four wheeler tippers, which were painted in their own distinctive livery. The Loanhead colours of Moorland Grey, Cream and Post Office Red were actually the same colours as the fleet of William Lind & Co Ltd. 'There was a big demand for stone,' recalled Bill Lind, 'so I bought a quarry at Loanhead from William Smith. I didn't really want to put any more trucks of my own fleet onto the road, but I approached Donald and asked him if he wanted to get involved with a new business. He agreed to take 60% of the equity and I had the other 40%. One of the first big jobs we did was to supply all the stone for the new Brodick pier on the Isle of Arran. The ferry people had to lay on an extra ferry – just for the tippers – but the wealth of work then available, meant the new vehicles were quickly paid for.'

To understand why Loanhead Transport was created (or even allowed) then you have to appreciate the irresistible dynamics of Donald Malcolm. Even on the day when he signed the business over to Grampian, Donald felt that he wanted to have some insurance: 'Just in case I have to walk away from Grampian and start again on my own,' he said.

Another contributing factor to the origins of Loanhead (plus the purchase & development of James Cunninghame and the later creation of Brookfield Securities with the diverse interests it included) involved the structure of being a subsidiary of Grampian. Historically, Malcolms have always used a huge number of sub contractors but often was the case - when Donald approached Grampian to buy more trucks – he was told there was no money for such investment. Donald's response was to ask if he could buy vehicles himself and then put them to work for WH Malcolm Ltd in the same way that sub-contractors were used.

The Grampian Board was consulted about such a move and agreement was given. Why – you might ask. The answer was simply that Donald Malcolm was proving to be a godsend to Grampian as year on year, the profits WH Malcolm Ltd were returning, grew ever larger. If he could continue doing that, what harm was there in letting him buy vehicles. The Group already uses sub-contractors, so what harm is there in sub-contracting Donald Malcolm.

The practical operation of Loanhead was slightly complicated in that WH Malcolm would bill Loanhead for fuel drawn, any servicing & repairs carried out and even paying for WH Malcolm drivers who may have been used on these vehicles, but everything was above board and transparent. When the quarry operation of William Lind & Co Ltd were sold to the Tarmac Group in 1972 (the Lind fleet of 10 vehicles were

sold off to WH Malcolm and Loanhead Transport) Bill Lind moved to a small office at Brookfield to look after the admin of Loanhead. Bill – and his secretary Delaine Colquhoun remained there until 1987 when Donald bought out Bill's share of Loanhead. However, Bill actually gifted his proceeds to an organisation called The Ballast Trust. With premises in Johnstone, The Ballast Trust exists solely to process technical archives and business records.

For tax purposes, arrangements were then made for Loanhead to be passed into the ownership of Donald's two sons - Walter & Andrew – plus a trust created for the Malcolm grandchildren.

JAMES CUNNINGHAME

When Grampian bought WH Malcolm Ltd in 1960 not all the assets of Marion & Donald Malcolm were bought. Obviously the Boghouse Farm wasn't part of the deal nor was Malcolm

When the Logan coal company was taken over by John Hudson, WH Malcolm were asked if they were interested in the contract hire operation of three dedicated tankers on heavy fuel oil. Frank Graham is the pictured driver while John Strang and Jim McNaught drove the two other similar outfits. The tankers were based in WH Malcolm's Cartside depot. Although the vehicles were operated through the Hudson office in Paisley, all the oil was collected from the Grangemouth terminal. In 2006, WH Malcolm operates one artic tanker (see page 104) but this is used purely to transfer vehicle fuel from the supplier at Clydebank to the Malcolm depots throughout the Scottish central belt.

Blaes Co. Ltd. Donald Malcolm had realised very early in his life how much money there could be in waste. So while some people may have looked at the various bings in the area (huge piles of burnt colliery waste) as a blot on the landscape, Donald looked at these as ideal sources of infill, especially when things like the M8 motorway was being built through the heart of Glasgow.

As an aside to this, Bert Brown also recalls the Paisley sanitary manufacturing concern of J&R Howie: 'Over the years, they'd built up a huge heap of reject wash basins and toilets etc which were piled up in a heap, but I remember Donald identifying this as being ideal for a hardcore type filler. So when Chrysler were looking to flatten their Linwood site prior to building their Hillman Imp car factory, Donald negotiated the disposal – on behalf of Howies – of all this waste sanitary ware. He was very astute in that respect.'

In March 1965, Grampian bought Malcolm Blaes Co Ltd and naturally Donald wanted to put the proceeds of the sale to good use. However, rather than just put it into the bank, Donald spotted a very good investment.

It's not known how he came across them but finding about 10 small vans based in the Gorbals area of Glasgow was like finding gold dust. The fleet in the name of James Cunninghame had been used – amongst other things – to deliver hats for the millinery trade. Donald had no interest in that line of work but it was the vehicle's 'A' licences (yes, on a fleet of small vans) that prompted the swift purchase of this company.

The vans were soon sold on but the licences were transferred onto larger goods carrying vehicles. This was an accepted practice but during the transition, Donald slowly upgraded the licence's specified unladen weight. Normally, you had to attend a hearing for major changes to the licence weights but nominal adjustments to these weights were rubber-stamped. And of course, astute Donald gradually upgraded these vehicles as they again went to work (as sub contractors) for WH Malcolm Ltd. In time, Grampian Holdings would buy the James Cunninghame fleet but not, of course, before their value went up.

Malcolm Plant Ltd was formed in 1965 primarily to acquire the business and assets of John Best, who at the time operated six earth-moving machines. Donald is seen second from the left – shaking hands with Duncan Grassie, Sales Director of Scottish Land Development (SLD). John Best is seen third from left in this hand over pose taken around February 1972. Brian Hatfield, Sales Manager of SLD is the figure on the far right. The machines were supplied through Scottish Land – as agents of Hy-Mac - although WH Malcolm general haulage drivers of old, can recall hauling these machines to Scotland from the Hy-Mac factory at Ryhmney in South Wales. It was apparently a work of art, but two of these 580c tracked excavators could be squeezed onto a standard 40' flat trailer. Malcolms bought their first Hy-Mac in 1965 while the machines were recalled favourably as they were reliable & reasonably cheap to run. One of these Hy-Mac 580c machines has been restored as part of the Malcolm preserved vehicle collection.

After the local carriers concern of Wilson Bros. (Haulage) Ltd was acquired in 1961, WH Malcolm inherited all manner of traffic for well-known, blue chip concerns. Heinz had this distribution depot on Scott Road in Paisley and a regular operation of Malcolms was to bring full loads in from the Heinz, Kitt Green factory at Wigan. The Malcolm local distribution motors – which worked out of Paisley - could be loaded with anything from 40-50 drops per day and these four wheelers normally carried a van boy with them. This wasn't just to help out with carrying the tins, cans and bottles, but also to enhance the load's security. To improve this aspect of the operation, Malcolms were early users of the curtain side type of bodywork (as seen) for this work.

James Cunninghame operated about 10 Fordson vans in the Gorbals area of Glasgow. But after Donald bought the vehicles – and their important 'A' licences – in 1966, he used the Cunninghame name as a dedicated form of sub contractor, albeit in corporate colours. By August 1977, James Cunninghame had 35 vehicles (and three trailers) listed on their Operators Licence. In the main these vehicles were tippers but some flat artics also carried the Cunninghame name. Also of note from the Operator's Licence records is that in 1979, there were 10 different companies listed as operating 365 vehicles (and 209 trailers) under the Grampian / Malcolm banner. This list included Donald himself who held a licence for 30 vehicles and 16 trailers at that time.

MALCOLM PLANT

Donald Malcolm was quick to weigh people up although occasionally he did get flummoxed. Admittedly he did like an argument although driver Willie Ballantyne's approach was very off putting: 'Whenever Donald used to rant & rave at me,' said Willie, 'I just used to stand and laugh at him. He didn't know what to make of me.'

Naturally most on the staff would simply let Donald have his say, as they knew he'd soon forget about the problem once he'd got it off his chest. However, in the form of John Best, Donald was to – almost – meet his match.

To his credit, John Best was a recognised expert in the field of Plant Hire and Donald accepted this. Malcolm Plant Ltd was formed – within Grampian – in June 1965 not only to take over the earth moving vehicles of WH Malcolm Ltd – and those acquired with the purchase of William Wilson & Son (Johnstone) Ltd - but also the six machines purchased with John Best Plant Hire. It was to be John Best's brief – assisted by Pat Callaghan – to develop the plant hire business while to assist those two, 23-year-old Jim Anderson was also recruited.

Malcolm Plant Ltd had their traffic office in Boghouse (until they moved to Murray Street in 1997) but to co-ordinate the use of the machines, the low loaders and the management, Pye two-way radios were fitted to as many vehicles /machines / cars as possible: 'I only had a motor bike then,' recalls Jim Anderson, 'but as well as the start off pay of £18 per week, I was also given a Mini pick up to use and this had a two way radio in as well.'

We take mobile phones for granted in 2006, but 40 years earlier, these Pye radios were the cutting edge of modern communication technology although there were drawbacks to them. If a radio handset slid down the seat, it was an easy mistake for the driver to sit on the transmit button and block out the rest of the network. Another problem was that Malcolm Plant had to share the Pye network with other users: 'I think Scotts the electricians of Glasgow were on the same network as us,' said Jim and it's also believed that a pharmaceutical company in Edinburgh (amongst others) could also hear the WH Malcolm transmissions if there were freak happenings with the atmospherics.

A number of base stations were part of the Malcolm system and what made things interesting (to the avid listeners of Malcolm Radio) were the times when Donald Malcolm and John Best would discuss the merits of one thing or another. John could give Donald just as good as he got and of course, this action could get Donald even more agitated. However, when these discussions on the finer points of life were heard in a variety of other offices (sharing the Pye radio network) across Scotland's Central Belt, there were naturally complaints made to the manufacturers of Pye.

Pye of course made Donald – as Chairman of WH Malcolm Ltd - aware of these 'terrible' complaints and of course he assured the radio concern that he would fully investigate the use of such foul language on the radio: 'I can assure you,' Donald told the Pye representative, 'that if I ever discover who these foul mouthed people are then I will deal with them in the severest manner.' With such an assurance, Pye obviously accepted that the matter was well in hand although they didn't realise they had been talking to one of the main protagonists.

The big problem with plant hire was that you had to be very fluid with its operation. It was a big selling point for WH Malcolm that contractors should hire both plant and tippers from Malcolms: 'If our machine goes off,' they told the prospective customer, 'then you don't have to pay for the tippers standing around waiting for the machine to be repaired.'

Limiting their general operating radius to within about 25 miles didn't seem that big but in practice, it was big enough when you realise how busy building work was in the Glasgow area and the plant fleet steadily grew. Never a buyer of the biggest machines, the Malcolm doctrine was to invest in the best earners but as machines could be taken off hire very quickly, it needed a quick response from the Malcolm low loader drivers to get it onto the next job: 'You've got to get it there before it's asked for,' was Donald's impossible demand.

Security of the machines was another big problem (when working in some parts of Glasgow) although some customers, like the railways, also needed Malcolms to work at the railway's quietest times – weekends and during the night. 'That could be a bit entertaining,' recalled Jim Anderson as something of an understatement. 'I remember one night there were two wedding parties going on – quiet close to each other. But when they started taking pot shots at each other with air rifles our crews were caught in the middle so we had to run the gauntlet and get out of there. Although it was the times when the rifles weren't air powered that things became really interesting.'

Also said to be interesting, was the day a bomb was dug out of the Monklands Canal when a section of the M8 was being built: 'This bomb got loaded onto a tipper so when it was discovered, it was quite exciting – you still encounter them even after this length of time.'

Jim Anderson was to spend almost 40 years with Malcolm Plant and became a director of this company. Of all the interesting jobs he was involved in, he still laughs at the many discussions between Donald (DJM) and John Best. 'Being attached to Boghouse, we had the pleasure of Donald's first visit after breakfast. Some mornings were better than others but if DJM and John fell out then the folk at Murray Street always blamed the Plant Office for causing Donald's bad temper. Perhaps the best tale of the two was when Donald came on the phone looking for John Best to be told he was out: 'Tell the f...ing so and so to phone me urgent when he comes in,' instructed Donald.

John Best came back and phones Donald.

DJM: 'Where the f... have you been Best?'
John: 'Getting my hair cut.'
DJM: 'Not in my time you don't.'
John: 'It grows in your time.'
DJM: 'It doesn't all grow in my time.'
John: 'I didn't get it all cut.'

There was silence from Donald and then a big laugh. When you worked for Donald Malcolm he could at times be beaten – but not often.

Even though many people thought the large number of blaes bings dotted round the Central Belt of Scotland – and down into Lanarkshire - were simply a blot on the landscape, Donald quickly identified how invaluable they could be. He created the company of Malcolm Blaes Co. Ltd and this was eventually sold to Grampian in 1965. The waste proved to be ideal when new roads were being built and shovel driver Willie Anderson recalls how he loaded 1 million tons from the Mauchline Bing when the Kilmarnock by-pass was being built. One of the two, bonneted Volvo six wheel tippers of Malcolms is seen in shot and Jim McGlynn recalls he drove this one. 'It was a smashing motor to drive although being fitted with a trailing axle meant it was prone to getting stuck.'

WH Malcolm have been operating low loaders for almost 50 years but LHS 236P is recalled as their first ever, real heavy haulage outfit. With Cummins 290 engine, the Atkinson Venturer 6x4 tractor unit had George Shields as its regular driver. Capable of about 65 tons gross operation, the Atkinson had a varied life. Bob Monoghan recalls being sent out to give assistance when it broke down one night. Bob took Malcolm's first big Mack wrecker but wasn't sure what to do: 'I didn't know if Donald just wanted the Atkinson tractor brought back for repair so in the end, I decided to hitch the Mack up to everything and I dragged the outfit some 15 miles to the open cast coal site where it was delivering its load. I suppose I was grossing around 80 tons which shows how strong that old Mack was.'

Loanhead Transport Ltd was a privately owned company formed in 1967 when Donald Malcolm and Bill Lind joined forces taking 60% / 40% respective shares in the business. Bill Lind recalls the first vehicles as being a quartet of Bedford KM four wheelers, although subsequent purchases were six and eight wheelers. Initially the vehicles were all parked up at Brookfield but as time evolved, the Loanhead fleet became a dedicated sub-contractor to WH Malcolm / Grampian. The vehicles were then simply operated as an integral part of the Malcolm operation. The quartet of Seddon Atkinson 300 six wheelers came from the batch of 18 such vehicles bought by Donald in 1978. Recalled as being particularly fast, they were also known to corkscrew their prop shafts into pieces. Loanhead generally also operated one artic and while it may have been fine for abnormal load work (as pictured in Ayrshire Metals with a trombone trailer) it could be a handful when operating on tipper / quarry work: 'We used to nickname the artic "The Boat",' said Bill Lind, 'as it could wallow all over the place.'

The Loanhead colours of Moorland Grey, Cream and Post Office Red were identical to those used in Bill Lind's other company, William Lind & Co. Ltd. Bill Lind remained involved until Donald bought his share out about 1987 although Loanhead Transport continued to operate – as a distinct part of the Malcolm operation – until the family sold the vehicles to Grampian in 2001. Malcolm Mortimore records some of the other Loanhead vehicles as: BHS 898X and JHS 31Y Scania 86 six wheelers; JHS 52Y Leyland Reiver six wheeler; C733 FHS, D503 and D601 MHS Volvo FL7 six wheelers; F351, 355 – 367 DHS Scania 93 six / eight wheelers; G939 NGD Mercedes 2421 six wheeler; H277 VHS MAN eight wheeler; H285 and 286 VHS and J856 EHS Scania 93 six wheelers.

As well as buying both Volvo and Scania very strongly in the late 60's and early '70s, Donald had a soft spot for the Atkinson chassis – with the Gardner engine – in both tractor unit and rigid eight-wheeler form. The line up of tractor units (bottom) is pictured just after Malcolms moved their general haulage vehicles into their new Cartside depot in 1969. The tipper / low loader line up is seen at Murray Street. Family holiday trips to Blackpool or Lytham St Anne's in that period were always an excuse to include a visit to the Atkinson factory at Walton-le-Dale, which was close to the newly opened Malcolm depot at Preston. The two drivers in the Defender eight wheelers (top) are believed to be Danny O'Neill and Roddy Nicholson.

CHAPTER 8

Working for Donald

Donald Malcolm may have been Founder & Chairman of WH Malcolm Ltd (amongst the many other titles he held) but after the 1960 sell out, the bottom line meant he was simply an employee of Grampian Holdings. If you believe that, you'll believe anything because no matter what you did in the Grampian / Malcolm organisation, there was one basic truth above anything else. You never worked for Donald Malcolm, you always worked with Donald Malcolm.

Even Bill Hughes, the Grampian Chairman & CEO accepted that Donald's love was the Malcolm business and giving him free rein was always best in the long run. Donald was elected to the main Grampian Board and expected to attend the regular Board meetings but his input was very measured. 'I think he only took an interest when road transport was being discussed,' recalls John Douglas, who became Company Secretary at Grampian. 'As a 6' tall individual who weighed over 20 stone, Donald was a dominant figure of a man and – if he wanted - could be very aggressive. At times he would display glints of badness when he would wind up other board members, but in the right hands, he was often a big pussy cat.'

At their peak, Grampian Holdings had interests in 28 different sectors of business, but even though he held a large number of shares in the parent, Donald was rarely interested in how these other sectors were fairing: 'I've seen his eyes glaze over when other board members were talking,' said John, 'and you could tell his mind was elsewhere. I think the only time I saw him get a bit excited was when he looked through the boardroom window and spotted one of the Malcolm tippers in the distance. Donald obviously reckoned the driver was doing something he shouldn't so he grabbed a phone and tore someone to pieces – the Board had never seen anything like it.'

But what did you get if you worked for Donald Malcolm? 'He was a person who believed if people worked for him you became a Malcolm person,' said Bill Hughes. 'If you backed him 100%, then he would give you the same support back. And once he trusted you as a Malcolm person, you knew you had job security for life.' And as it was Donald's policy that no one was ever forced into retirement at 65 or earlier (a ruling which still holds today) staff knew the Big Man would ensure there was a job for them, for as long as they wanted.

However, Donald's way of working didn't suit everyone. When Jack Semple was interviewing Donald for a feature in Truck Magazine during 1987, Donald was pleased to say he'd never made anyone redundant but admitted that the turnover of staff was somewhat erratic: 'Among managers, staff turnover is virtually non-existent,' said Donald. 'Among drivers it was 110% one year – but that was because the bottom 10% of drivers would come and go 10 times.'

A DRIVERS LOT

Yes, there were some drivers who came and went at Malcolms but there were many others that simply came and stayed. Willie Ballantyne joined Donald Malcolm in 1951 and stayed with him for 44 years. Willie had just done his National Service so moving half track, 25 pounder guns with the Royal Artillery was good enough driving experience for Donald. 'Donald ran a mix of four wheeled tippers back then,' said Willie, 'including some four wheel drive Canadian Fords which could do all sorts of off road work. It was Donald's instructions that if a customer wanted a motor somewhere, then we were to get it there. He always tried to please his customers, that's why we got so much work. He never refused a job and Donald always insisted, you didn't finish

Of all the material carried by Malcolm tippers, the haulage of sulphur from the dock at Ardrossan to ICI's plant at Stevenston was particularly testing. Due to the hazardous nature of the product, the driver had to stay away from the vehicle during the loading, or at least keep the cab windows shut because the product could certainly: 'nip your eyes,' as one old driver described it, so eyewash facilities were always available. An operator was also on hand with a hosepipe because if the loading grab struck any metal, it was possible to create a flash fire with the sulphur powder. The Kilwinning based Harry Aitken usually drove CHS 24J although the Ayrshire depot were also allocated the similar four wheel Albion Clydesdale tippers CHS 25 and 26J. After they were loaded, vehicles had to be sheeted while drivers had to wear goggles & overalls while on this job. One bonus of this job being they were paid 'dirty money.'

Alex Brodie served a total of 23 years in his two stints with WH Malcolm. He has fond memories of the brand new Albion Reiver XHS 447H that he was given in 1970 when based at Kilwinning: 'It wasn't very fast and it was very noisy, but it was a good puller and I thought it was great.' Of all the traffic he was given, Alex recalls he seemed to get regular loads of sand: 'I'd load up at the Shawalton quarry in Irvine with sand for various foundries around Paisley and Falkirk and then back load out of the Alexandria quarry near Luss on the side of Loch Lomond. That was usually for delivery to Hulme Pipes back in Irvine – it was a great arrangement.'

until the customer said you were finished.'

Willie recalls a lot of back breaking shovelling in those earliest days: 'There were a couple of flax mills and the lace factory in Johnstone plus different boiler houses in Paisley that you took coal to every day – I've seen me hand shovel 40-50 tons of coal a day.' It was luxury indeed – for the Malcolm drivers – when Donald invested in mechanised loaders to work the waste blaes bings because some of these could be so hot, they had to be hosed down before they could be loaded.

In the earliest days, it's not surprising to hear how Willie describes Malcolms as very much a family business, as this first name approach of Donald with all his staff (and they back to him) lasted as long as Donald lived: 'Yes, Donald loved an argument and I think he sacked me twice but I was only finished for about half an hour. He was a good boss and very fair but you could argue back when he shouted at you. Donald always expected you to be early for work in the morning but his office door was always open – no matter what sort of problem you had. Although I can

remember Donald's mother putting him in his place at Brookfield when she thought it was merited. "Donald, you should never forget that YOU are working for ME," Granny Malcolm would say to him, with a twinkle in her eye. She was a great woman who got on with everyone and I'm sure Donald worshipped her - it was a big loss to many people when she died.'

In his time, Willie did all sorts of jobs but he reckoned the worst job was when he was on for the local Renfrewshire council spreading ash on the icy roads during the winter months: 'We used to carry two men in the back of the tipper and they had to shovel the ash out and spread it across the road. But as you could only drive at 5mph you were sat in the cab freezing while they were sweating with the general exertion of the job.'

The waste product of power station / boiler house ash made up some of Donald's earliest bulk loads and Willie recalls it as being one of the most versatile products you could imagine: 'I've seen it built into 9" thick layers and once it's been compacted down, it's harder than concrete.'

They may not have stayed very long – and there were only six of them – but the Russian Belaz dumpers, that came to Malcolms in the mid 1970s left a big impression with anyone who ever had dealings with them. Bill Lind – of Loanhead Transport – describes them as having a turning circle like a paddle steamer. Jim Anderson of Malcolm Plant recalls how they required a 15-mile detour just because they couldn't get round one particular corner enroute to Hunterston Power Station. Supplied through Sam (Moore) Plant, the first three Belaz 256Bs came (with an individual price tag of £11,000) between May and October 1975 while the other three came in November & December 1976. Freddie McAllister recalls they had poor brakes, while the only good thing about them was they were huge - everyone else on the road seemed to get out their way. They had all been sold on by May 1979 but although known as Belaz, the 256Bs were actually built by another Soviet Union manufacturer, Kraz, but sold into the UK under the Belaz name. Giving far better service to Malcolm Plant were the 13 AEC Dumptruk 6x4s, which were bought between August 1966 and July 1970. They were all sold by March 1978.

Tidysite was a small Glasgow based waste disposal concern brought into the Grampian / Malcolm fold during 1973 primarily to acquire the name. With chrome bumper and V8 Perkins engine, this Ford D Series (above) was the pride & joy of Murray Street based Jock McLean. Jock was a big friend of Donald and is recalled as being quite a handyman who also kept his own smallholding near Johnstone. The four wheel rigid was the standard skip carrying motor of the era, so when Malcolms introduced a six wheel Leyland Reiver into skip carrying work, it gave them a big step up on the competition. Jimmy Little usually drove this vehicle, which had Shepherd Miller skip carrying equipment.

As the years passed, Willie went from Canadian Fords, to Bedfords, Albion Reivers to Leylands and MANs, then in latter years to Volvos and Scanias. Perhaps the oddest tipper job, which Willie did, was carrying waste copper: 'I'd load during the afternoon but had to put the truck inside the garage and go home for a kip. I would start again around 12 midnight and was expected to make Liverpool – or wherever – in one hit. You couldn't leave a load like this stood on a café car park. After tipping the copper, you'd get a back load of sand – it was really a good job.'

One thing Willie recalls is that Donald would pay whatever overtime you worked: 'He paid Union rates - or just above - and it was double time on a Sunday. If you were prepared to work it, Donald was always prepared to pay it.'

Willie's last thoughts on Donald: 'I don't think there was another boss like him in the country, as he'd do anything for anybody. I remember seeing a pile of Council House rent books on his desk and these were from guys who somehow couldn't sort their finances out. Donald made sure their rent was paid and although it later came out of their wages, Donald got a lot of people out of a lot of scrapes and few people really knew about all the things he used to do and pay for – and not get his money back. Even during the big national drivers strikes in the 1970s when we were out for weeks, Donald was all for paying what the men wanted as he wanted them back at work. A lot of drivers thought very highly about him for that. If you were a Malcolm man and in any bother, Donald would help you out.'

VIEW FROM THE GARAGE

While there have always been legal limits on how long drivers can work, these limits never applied to the garage (or admin) staff – and Donald certainly knew that. But again, if you worked overtime, you were paid for it although if you ever accepted the move up to staff – or the dizzy heights of a directorship – this simply meant you didn't get paid for those extra hours. The huge rise in salary on promotion (or so Donald thought) was enough recompense: 'And don't forget, as a director you also get a company car.'

In the earliest of days, Malcolm drivers like Charlie Galbraith and Jimmy Kilpatrick used to stay back on a night and do the vehicle repairs, but as the business expanded, the workshops side of the company became hugely significant for operational efficiency. Malcolms didn't know the meaning of the words – spare vehicles – because if a motor was fit for work, then it shouldn't be in

The Volvo F7 eight-wheel rigid tipper was bought in large numbers as Donald reckoned it was his favourite motor. It's recalled as being a very good performer – especially the way it could get in and out of the soft. Fitted with a coal carrying Edbro Fastline body, Tommy Glen is believed to be the pictured driver. Before Volvo ever built their first eight wheel rigid for the UK market at Irvine (the F86) Malcolm driver George McTaggart was asked to take the Scammell Routeman eight wheel rigid – he was then driving – to the Irvine factory. Apparently the vehicle stayed there for two days while the Volvo engineers studied the steering geometry used for the two front axles – prior to designing their own.

The first ever WH Malcolm curtainsider semi-trailer into service in the mid 1970s was this Southfields Hustler and it was to herald the eventual demise of the standard flat. In 2006, of the 987 semi-trailers owned by the company, 802 now have curtainsider bodywork. The balance is made up of skeletals, CLVs (crown locked vans) one tanker trailer plus 40 flats. Making less of an inroad into the WH Malcolm operation was the marque of Mercedes-Benz. Drivers of these early models complained that their brakes were never any good and they didn't really pull very well. This 1924 model tractor unit was new in 1975, while the records of John Mollett shows the only other Mercs of the era being a similar tractor unit LHS 242P and the six wheel rigid flat, LHS 244P.

John Mollett's archives record the first MAN to join the WH Malcolm fleet as the 4x2 tractor unit UHS 474M which Frank Murney was given. With sleeper cab – and distinctive steering column mounted gear lever – the tractor was taken as a seed vehicle. It did so well that Donald gave a big order for a mix of MAN tractor units and eight wheelers which came into service during early 1976. Donald was to have a very good rapport with Cannis Duffy, the principal of the supplying MAN dealer MITM. No prizes for identifying the 'shadow' of a figure at the wheel of this tipper.

the yard. And those in the traffic office had hell to pay if vehicles weren't being utilised properly.

The pressure was on the mechanics & garage staff to carry out any repairs that were required and to that end, all manner of spares were kept in the Malcolm stores. And if the repairs weren't done or the stores ran out of spares, then the Big Man sounding off made sure you didn't make that mistake again.

Although the company has operated their own breakdown vehicles for many years, in the early days it was expected that mechanics would go and repair the relevant vehicle – wherever it broke down. Dave McLune (who became foreman mechanic at the Kilwinning depot) recalls his longest run for a repair was to be near Otterburn in Northumberland: 'Donald always insisted it was cheaper if we went out and repaired our own vehicles and if we did them ourselves, we knew the repairs were done properly.'

Dave had to borrow depot manager Jim Paterson's car for this run and he ended up doing the repairs by moonlight. 'I think I eventually got home about lunch time - just in time to get a wash and go back to work.'

When Dave joined Malcolms in 1968 it was company policy to park all the Kilwinning vehicles inside the Woodwynd garage: 'We only stopped doing that after a four wheel Seddon flat caught fire – after an electrical problem - when parked for the night. Fortunately it was confined to the Seddon cab – but it could have spread to all the vehicles parked inside.' That motor was normally driven by William Shanks who left Kilwinning every week doing 20-30 drops around Devon & Cornwall carrying sanitary ware for the aptly named Shanks concern.

Kilwinning had a mix of tippers and flats, which gave Dave McLune (and his apprentice Robert Walker) a variety of jobs to do. When you're working as a mechanic you don't see much excitement, but Dave recalls the day when a loaded four wheeler drove into the yard with the rear hub on fire: 'Obviously the brake was hanging on and the driver hadn't been aware of what was happening. But as it was loaded with some specialist aviation type fuel from Shell, I ran out with a fire extinguisher and put the fire out before too much damage was caused.' You have to be a cool customer to work at Malcolms.

Kilwinning was ideally placed for the huge variety of traffic generated in this part of Ayrshire so its no surprise the company expanded to new, purpose built premises – on Nethermains Road –

about 1974: 'I think the place was originally an old piggery on the side of an ironworks site but to us, when the new garage was built it was like moving to paradise.'

Amongst the fleet at Kilwinning, Malcolms operated 10 artic tippers that primarily carried Ayrshire sourced coal all over the country. But this traffic stopped in the early days of the 1984 Miners Strike: 'We were told if we didn't stop carrying coal then all the other Malcolm trucks running into the likes of Shell and ICI would be blacked. So Donald told us to stop and the artic tipping trailers were just parked up.'

Dave worked at Malcolms Kilwinning depot until the day he retired in December 2002: 'It wasn't a job I had,' said Dave, 'it was a lifestyle. When you worked for Donald, you were totally committed as you'd do anything for him - only occasionally did I get a Sunday off. Donald liked his pound of flesh but you got paid for it. And even if he fell out with you one minute, he would then turn round and give you a sub if you were in trouble. Yes, he was a hard taskmaster but he'd never pass anyone in the depot without having a word with them. And he was always ready to listen to what you wanted to say. He could change his mind if you thought your way was better – it wasn't just his way all the time.'

Dave may have had plenty work to do at Kilwinning but guys like Billy Kirkpatrick will probably say he was having a picnic compared to life at Murray Street. Billy joined WH Malcolm (when still at Brookfield) in 1963 as an apprentice and 42 years on he's still with the company. 'I always remember Donald as a very approachable sort of guy,' said Billy. 'He told me right at the outset that you could always speak to him no matter what the problem was.'

The Murray Street depot was built from scratch in a vacant plot next to Irvine Caravans and the garage staff moved there in 1964. Billy even did a stint – at weekends – helping out Dave McLune at Kilwinning although he was to be promoted Night Shift Foreman at Murray Street – a job he had for 18 years.

Think of any mechanical job you like – right up to complete vehicle rebuilds - and the Malcolms garage staff could certainly do it - The Big Man expected nothing else. Overtime was generally considered as compulsory and when you joined Malcolms you had to appreciate that Christmas Day was just another working day.

Through the years, Donald got excellent service from the marque of Albion – and especially the Clydesdale and Reiver models – but as the name was phased out in favour of Leyland, less of these UK built vehicles were bought. John Mollett records a pair of Leyland Marathon tractor units – WHS 184S (which Trevor Garrod drove) and 186S - came into service in late 1977, but the only real noteworthy Leyland acquisition was when Donald bought a batch of about 16 Clydesdale four wheelers in the mid 1980s. This is believed to have been a cancelled export order (for Africa), but as it was thought they might be broken up for spare parts, they all received Coventry 'Q' plate registrations (indicating their date of manufacture was unknown). Malcolm Mortimore records Q240-242 GVC and Q978 and 979 GRW as being four-wheel tippers. Freddie McAllister recalls they all came in long wheelbase, chassis cab form and had to be cut down for tipper use. The box van Clydesdale was used for the multi-drop Heinz shop delivery work.

THE MANAGERS VIEW

Life can be stressful – depending on your personal makeup – but some of the old Malcolm managers will tell you that you didn't know the meaning of the word 'Stress' unless you'd worked for Donald Malcolm. Bert Brown recalls one conversation when he was telling someone he was due to get a watch after doing 25 years service with Malcolms: 'A gold watch?' the response apparently was. 'If you've done 25 years for Donald Malcolm you should be getting the Victoria Cross'

There was no such thing as a 9-5 job with Malcolm's management team as even the white shirts worked long hours and weekends. This was the company which Peter Strachan joined in November 1968 after he'd answered an advert for an Earth Moving Operations Manager: 'The first time I came to Malcolms,' said Peter, 'I remember liking the feel of the place. As a car buff, I noticed there were quite a few Mercedes cars parked in the yard so it suggested that Malcolms were on a sound financial footing.'

Although Peter Strachan was just one new employee, the way he developed his job would be the key to a huge amount of Company employment – and also the key to why the current Malcolm Construction Services Division is doing so well. 'There was a trend just starting in the late '60s for civil engineers to ask contractors for a complete package. They were perhaps after a site clearing or preparing to construct a new building and as Malcolms ran both plant & tippers, we could then sell them the deal to manage whatever was required. Obviously contracts varied but generally it was to a fixed cost and it took away the worry – from them – of the various problems of weather, machine failure or even tippers not arriving or perhaps leaving without a full load. When they gave the job to us, we did it all.'

When Peter now drives round the Greater Glasgow area, he identifies all manner of buildings which Malcolms started: 'I'd sometimes be running up to four jobs at the same time,' said Peter, 'but the extension of the Wiseman Dairy bottling plant at Bellshill, was probably my biggest. I think we moved 30,000 cubic metres of spoil out of there.'

It helped a huge amount, if Peter had good machine operators working for him and – from memory – he speaks highly of Davy Mulroy, Jimmy Alan and John Smith: 'John normally drove a Cat 977 and he could level – by eye -

something the size of a football pitch to within an inch – he was simply an artist.'

Where Malcolms won work (in favour of other contractors) was because they could dispose of the material: 'We had a chain of tips around the area which we could use,' explains Peter, 'and I've even seen earth tipped onto a farmer's land where they have asked Donald if he could level out the depression in their field.'

Keeping abreast of what you could do with the excavated materials saw Malcolms sell on the sand they discovered when excavating the Anderson Cross development. While whenever boulder clay was discovered, Peter knew the British Waterways would take that for sealing their various canals across Scotland's Central Belt.

Of all the Managers at Malcolms, the main reason that Peter differed from the rest was because he never fell out with Donald: 'I remember talking to him when we were waiting to see someone about a job and he asked how long I'd worked for him. I told him then it was 22 years (he went on to serve 30 years at Malcolms) and this surprised Donald slightly. "Do you realise that in all that time we've never had an argument – I'd better send that fact to the Guinness Book of Records."'

With such a good working relationship, it's not surprising that Peter has fond memories of Donald: 'I suppose to start with he made me suffer from shock, awe and admiration – often at the same time. But you have to admire the man who built this empire from nothing as no one worked harder than him – he literally worked day & night. The job was his hobby and his life while he had such a brain & memory. He could keep track of whatever was going on all the time and while he worked you hard, he was fair. I had great respect for the man.'

Peter required a number of big medical operations in the mid '80s and even when he came back to work, he recalls Donald being particularly considerate: 'The boys say you don't look well,' he said to Peter one day on the phone. Peter said he was fine but Donald wouldn't have it: 'Don't start until 9.30am and then go home at lunch time – just work like that until you get a bit stronger.'

You could say Donald's approach to Peter (and many others on the staff who had suffered someway) was just basic consideration. You could also see how Donald was simply looking after one of the team that had done so well for him. This approach was part of the package when you became Malcolmised.

Container based traffic – especially linked to their rail network – is currently a major part of the Malcolm workload. However, the company has been moving this form of traffic for more than 30 years. Pictured at the Containerbase terminal at Coatbridge, this Volvo F86 was based at the company's Castlebank Street depot. The F86 proved a good servant to Malcolms as the company also bought it in rigid, six-wheeler form. Doing multi-drop work for the likes of Weir Pumps proved the necessity of having such a versatile form of vehicle in your fleet.

Of all the motors operated by WH Malcolm, the ones driven by Gordon McDonald always seemed to look a shade better. 'I always looked after my wagon,' said Gordon who did almost 40 years with the company before retiring. His first F88 was YHS 651H and he then got MHS 953L: 'It was only a 240,' said Gordon, 'but it never let me down.' As you can see by the extra badges on THS 295R, Gordon's last F88 – a 290 – his unit did look the part. Whenever Gordon was due to go on holiday, he'd drive his truck from Cartside to Brookfield and park it out the way – so no one else could drive it while he was away. Gordon recalls this last F88 had the potential to reach 75mph although one regret was Donald would never buy him an exterior sun visor: 'I even offered to pay half the cost but Donald said if I got one, then everyone else would want one.'

The very close relationship between WH Malcolm and the Volvo factory at Irvine meant that when Volvo wanted someone to quietly run their first prototype FL6, then it was given to Malcolms. Jim Paterson, Kilwinning manager, recalls this first test vehicle – a left hand drive, four-wheel tipper - was painted all white. 'It had no Volvo markings at all,' said Jim, 'and was actually registered with Irish plates. Peter Dawkins usually drove that vehicle.' F302 DHS is one of the subsequent production models, which Jimmy Simpson usually drove. It's fitted with Edbro skip lifting equipment.

The versatility of the WH Malcolm heavy haulage section is shown with this Caterpillar powered Foden 6x4 unit. Kitted out with a ballast box on the back, it hauled a pair of independent dollies on long length, fabrication work. WH Malcolm moved most of Whiteinch Demolition machines and in 1991, the German built Liebherr 942 was classed by them as a very big machine. Tipping the scales around the 45 tons mark, it had Robert Wright as its usual operator. The Whiteinch work took their machines – and the WH Malcolm low loaders - all over Scotland.

CHAPTER 9

Donald and his Shadow

The 1968 Transport Act was to have a big effect on the development of WH Malcolm Ltd. With the introduction of 'O' Operators Licensing, the massive value of the Company's hard fought for 'A' licences was dismissed at a stroke. However, no longer would Grampian have to continue buying up companies, simply for their important Carriers licences. As it then became a – fairly – simple matter to have as many vehicles as you wanted on your 'O' licence, just by asking for them.

One small company which WH Malcolm did buy in the early 1970s – primarily for their name - was that of Tidysite. WH Malcolm first got into skip hire (rather modestly) in the late 1960s when the first skip loader and 20 skips were purchased. Within a few years, this work had expanded to employ eight vehicles and 300 skips working around Glasgow and Renfrewshire on industrial waste disposal.

In the early 1970s, WH Malcolm even considered building their own incinerator to dispose of combustible industrial refuse. But when it was announced that Local Authorities would take primary responsibility for all incinerators, these plans had to be shelved.

HORSES FOR COURSES

On paper, the growth in numbers of the Malcolm fleet during the 1970s wasn't as massive as the previous decade but that is slightly misleading. With the maximum weight of artics jumping from 24 to 32 tons gross, the carrying capacity of the company vehicles increased markedly. The change to Operators licensing also allowed Malcolms to upgrade both their rigid flat and tipper fleet (without having to ask permission) so if their practical operation allowed, four wheelers were phased out and replaced with six or eight wheel rigids of greater carrying capacity.

With such a huge and varied operation, it's not surprising that Malcolms operated so many different makes of truck. Their one common denominator being that Donald generally bought them all as he proved to be one very shrewd businessman when it came to driving a hard bargain. Transport journalist Jack Semple recalls one incident which Phil Ridgeway recounted. 'I got to be good friends with Donald,' said Phil, 'but I complained to him one day how he never bought any trucks from me. I was selling ERFs at that time but Donald turned round and said, "You are a friend – that's exactly why I won't buy any trucks from you."'

Andrew Malcolm doesn't think the inference in that recollection is totally true: 'My Dad was very much a people person and he liked the personal relationships he had with all our suppliers. He could be very aggressive but he was also very loyal.' And Donald Malcolm was of the school where a handshake meant everything and once he'd given his word, that was his bond.

The Malcolm fleet lists of old reflect the huge variety of vehicles which Donald bought – usually new - but sometimes second hand. He had a good relationship with Jim McKelvie (who set up the importing of Volvos through Ailsa Trucks after he'd sold McKelvie Transport to the Transport Development Group) but had mixed feelings about Scania. 'He told me that he had a love / hate relationship with Scania,' recalled Jack Semple, 'as he reckoned they never knew what to charge for them.'

But even after he'd bought some vehicles, Donald wasn't averse to try and extract even more from the deal. When Jim Lamont (of Ailsa Trucks) called one Friday to collect a cheque (for around £300,000 to pay for a batch of Volvos) Donald handed it over but insisted he took Jim out for lunch. After the lunch, Donald also insisted that Jim came back into his Murray Street

The late Willie Ballantyne always reckoned that he gave Andrew his first driving lesson – at the age of two. But ever since, Andrew has driven anything and everything, which came into the Malcolm fleet. He practised his manoeuvring art with this weathered Thames Trader tractor unit. Originally used as a shunter at the Cartside depot, it was moved up to the Brookfield yard where Andrew adopted it for himself. The task he set himself was always straightforward – pick a trailer up, move it somewhere else and then put it down. Never has one Thames Trader moved so many trailers, in one small space.

office for a cup of tea: 'I've got to go,' said Jim who wanted to get the cheque into the bank before it closed at 3.30pm. Donald obviously knew this, but insisted that Jim had several cups of tea and he kept the conversation going until almost 3.30pm. There was no chance of Jim then making the standard banking deadline but Donald was taken aback when he found out later the cheque did go through on that Friday afternoon. 'How did you manage that,' he later asked Jim. 'I knew what you'd do so I'd arranged with the Bank Manager for him to stay open until 4pm - just so I could get your cheque cleared.' Another hearty laugh from the Big Man.

THE SHADOW

Donald was always his own man but being very much a people person, he also always liked to have friends and family around him. From about 1967, he also always seemed to have a shadow: 'Ever since I was about 4 or 5 years old,' recalled Andrew Malcolm, 'I used to spend every spare minute I had with my Dad. People used to say that Donald wouldn't go anywhere without his shadow but really as well as being my father, he became my best friend as well.'

While his elder brother Walter soon found the sport of rugby to excel in, Andrew instead preferred the Brookfield yard as his playground and as soon as he could reach the pedals, he could be found driving everything from a Mini to a 32 ton MAN artic round the yard. 'I think I was 30 before I had any other interests or hobbies apart from the WH Malcolm business,' he said.

As long as he had his Shadow with him, Donald wouldn't need to try out anything for himself: 'I remember going down to Stoke-on-Trent with my Dad,' recalled Andrew, 'to buy a second hand Towmaster. And when the salesman asked Donald to try it out, my Dad said that I would do it. The guy was a bit surprised but by then, my Dad knew that if I said a vehicle was OK, then it was good enough for him.'

When the Paisley & Renfrewshire Gazette came to record a huge order of new MANs being delivered to WH Malcolm in February 1976, it was to be the 14 year old Andrew who gave the reporter a demonstration drive round the yard – and a lesson of how easily the new MANs could be reversed. No wonder the banner headline read – with an inference of surprise: 'A boy can drive them.'

Obviously school took first call on the youngest Malcolm's time but school holidays and weekends were when his unofficial apprenticeship was carried out. This didn't just involve being able to drive – anything and

In February 1976, Donald bought his first big batch of MANs. With the order being worth £220,000, the supplying dealer – MITM – wanted to involve the local press with the news. Naturally, when the Paisley & Renfrewshire Gazette reporter wanted someone to demonstrate the new MANs in motion, 14-year-old Andrew was just the one to do it. Handing over the keys to Donald is Alec Thomas while George Richmond is stood on the left next to Andrew.

By the time Andrew had reached the age of 16 (above) he'd out grown Donald. But thanks to the Young Driver's Scheme, it wouldn't be long before Andrew could legally take an HGV onto the open road. Two different – second hand – Leyland Clydesdales were his first vehicles – HEN 318N and OHS 226P. His first six-wheeler, was the weathered Volvo F86 – NXS 446L – so it was a big day when the brand new F7 – RHS 567W – arrived for Andrew. Like all the earlier vehicles which he personalised, the livery includes the wording 'Isle of Lewis' as a reminder of Granny Malcolm's roots. However, it was rather fitting because the variety of loads carried on this Volvo took Andrew out to all parts of the Western Isles. 'I carried a lot of the Shell specialist fuels out of Ardrossan,' said

Andrew, 'but the only way I could get onto one very small ferry was if we cut 2' off the length of the Volvo's body – it was that tight a squeeze.'

everything – but Andrew also learnt a lot about the business and how his father kept track of every vehicle they owned & whether it was still cost effective to keep in service. 'There was no set policy as to how long we'd keep a truck or a trailer,' explained Andrew. 'Dad used to keep everything in his little black book and he would know which vehicles were costing too much to repair. He'd go through it every Sunday and make sure it was kept up to date but really he knew by heart all the registrations of the vehicles we had – and even the ones we'd sold. I still do the same sort of thing he did – the only difference is that I use a bigger book and it's kept in the office, not in my pocket.'

The weekends at Malcolms were generally taken at a gentler pace, although last port of call after the Saturday run round the depots (when heading home to Brookfield from the Murray Street HQ) was always the Broadway café in Johnstone – and always for the same collection. Two boxes of King Edward cigars - to see Donald through the coming week - and of course, an ice cream cornet for the Shadow.

WRONG PLACE, RIGHT TIME

It was regularly said about Donald Malcolm that he could often be in the wrong place, at the right time. His passion for getting out to see his staff at work meant he could appear at any hour – day or night - in any part of the Malcolm domain asking how things were going. It didn't even matter that Donald may have been enroute somewhere else because if he spotted one of his vehicles in trouble, then he'd be the first to go and help. 'We were going to someone's wedding,' recalled his wife Wilma, 'and Donald was wearing a morning suit. But that still didn't stop him getting out when he saw one of the Malcolm vehicles broken down – and of course, he'd be the one to crawl underneath. He was impossible like that.'

Donald loved to drive and while his early runabouts may have been small cars like an Austin A35 (something he had an awful squeeze to get into and could only drive it if he hung his arm out of the window) he'd soon progressed to bigger Rovers and finally – his favourite – Mercedes. No log book (or tachograph) is required when you are driving a car and Donald

After spending a year or two with one of the smaller Malcolm vehicles, Andrew was to cut his low loader teeth doing the occasional trip with the company's largest outfit. To replace his Atkinson Venturer 6x4 (seen on page 63) George Shields was given this left hand drive Mack although it wasn't long before Frank Murney became its regular driver. Frank was probably one of the smallest drivers on the Malcolm staff so he loved piloting the company's biggest head turning outfit. He wasn't too keen on changing the strange American wheels but recalls the Mack for its huge internal engine hump and two massive bunks. With this NCK machine onboard, the outfit is probably grossing around 90 tons. Carrying all sorts of equipment to all parts of the UK, Frank recalls the tightest squeeze anywhere was always getting through the arch at Inverary – or over the hump back bridge there.

would often drive all manner of hours – usually in a brisk manner – with a variety of consequences. Donald's wife Wilma recalls one night, before they were married, of him falling asleep at the wheel of his car near Dumbarton and only waking up when he drove into a ditch.

However, the worst smash he had was when he took a short cut down the Johnstone by-pass – before it was fully opened. Donald had done this trick before during daylight hours (using the excuse that he was checking up on his men and the state of the construction work's progress) but on the night in question, he didn't know that someone had tipped a huge amount of stone on the nearly finished carriageway. With the open road to himself, Donald could have been touching 100mph but came to a halt when his Mercedes crashed into the stockpile. The collision pushed the Merc's engine and gearbox straight back through the passenger compartment although it was the state of the car's steering wheel, which beggared belief. Donald's ability to absorb the pressure of the smash meant the steering wheel was twisted simply by the strength of his arms.

How the big man walked away from that is simply down to his awesome strength but once he'd arranged for a Malcolm Plant vehicle to pick the wreck up, take it up to Brookfield and then cover it with a tarpaulin, delayed shock saw his knees finally buckle. The following few days were spent in bed although the bruising that covered Donald's body finally subsided. And while his physical strength saw him through that medical calamity, there was one fight that he would not win.

C739 (and C740) FHS were a brace of day cab Volvo F10 6x2 tractor units. Seen loaded with 3 large concrete sewer pipes (believed from Hulme Pipes at Irvine) the Kilwinning based Volvo is coupled to a Montracon extendable semi-trailer. As the 600 fleet numbering suggests, this was one of 15 similar 40'- 60' trombone semi-trailers Malcolms had at that time.

This Commer / Dodge D964 TBM was the company's first purpose built road sweeper and as soon as Donald asked Jimmy Donnelly to give it a test drive, Jimmy became known as the company brush man. Coming second hand - and painted in Go Plant's colours - it was always known as the Go-Go vehicle although Jimmy also recalls he was always being asked to go there and then go somewhere else. Jimmy did 30 years with Malcolms before retiring in 2001 with his last sweeper being R817 CHS.

Robert English began his transport career back in 1951 when Mathew Wilson of Wilson Brothers, Canal Street, Johnstone gave him a job and 55 years later, he's still at work for the Malcolm Group. Robert's first motor was a Morris Commercial four wheeler and local work for Wilsons could mean anything up to 40 drops on board. Robert became one of the first company artic drivers but those first Scammell semi-trailers are recalled for poor brakes: 'I've seen us unhitch and the trailers run away from you if you forgot to chock them.' Once Wilsons became part of WH Malcolms (in 1961) Robert was given all sorts of brand new motors to drive including the Scania 112 D523 MHS (above). However, if you ask which – out of all those vehicles – was the best, then he'll say it was the Foden F435 DHS (below): 'It was absolutely great,' he says.

Malcolm's first recovery vehicle fitted with hydraulic rams was this ex Army Mack. Bob Monoghan recalls flying down to Manchester in the late 1970s, then getting the bus to the Merrick premises at Heywood before driving the Cummins engine Mack back to Paisley. Freddie McAllister has fond memories of the huge cab, although his modest stature meant he could hardly see over the steering wheel when he was driving. The two original rear mounted posts protruding skywards had to be chopped down, as they tended to foul on the low bridges around Glasgow. With front mounted winch, the Mack was quite a performer but Bob recalls problems with the brakes. 'The transmission parking brake was useless,' he said, 'so one day when the weld on the air tank blew open and the foot brake failed, the only way I could stop was to drive into a pile of road chippings.'

To Trevor Booth – who joined the garage staff at Malcolms in 1987 - the 1976 R Series Mack Q203 RDS was his pride & joy. 'I loved driving that motor,' he said. 'It could only do 48mph, but it would do that up hill and down dale.' Trevor got as far as the Tay Bridge near Dundee doing recoveries with the twin Holmes 750 equipped motor. Bought from Newbridge Recovery in the early 1980s it did good service for Malcolms. Recalled as having a six-speed gearbox, it also had six reverse gears as well. Although sold on to the local Scania dealer, the Mack has stood the test of time as Trevor says M8 Recovery at Hillington, Glasgow, are now making use of it. Stood behind the Mack is another distinctive Malcolm wrecker of the period, an ex Swedish Army Magirus-Deutz. Having something like a V10 air-cooled engine – which gave it an awesome sound - the Maggie also had a very good winch: 'It was strong enough to pull the Queen Mary,' reckoned Freddie McAllister.

During the 1980s, Andrew Malcolm loved to have all manner of projects on the go and these photographs show the results of those efforts. Although having a Scania 111 cab, the massive 6x6 Q82 RDS (top right) started life as a Leyland Martian – with Rolls Royce petrol engine. Built for the Army as an all terrain mobile crane, Andrew bought it through a military surplus dealer at Girvan. Affectionately known as 'The Mongrel,' Andrew also transplanted a Scania engine & gearbox into the chassis. It was still dreadfully slow – and also heavy on the half shafts – so when required to work, it was far quicker to low loader it around. The winch it carried, however, was described as phenomenal: 'When a dozer got stuck in the Clyde,' said Andrew, 'it really showed how it could work.' Far quicker was Q277 PDS, although having a Volvo F86 cab, actually started life as a 4x4 AEC Matador. It was also fitted with a Volvo F86 engine and gearbox that gave it the potential of 40mph. It did quite a lot of work for Malcolms proving versatile enough to carry a snowplough. Both these wreckers were later cut up although the 111 cab from 'The Mongrel' is being re-cycled into the restoration of DHS 71T – Jim Marshall's vehicle when new.

Looking through Andrew Malcolm's photographs of the 1980s shows how busy their heavy haulage outfits were at that time. After a few years service as the top, heavy hauler, the Mack (featured on page 85) was replaced with the Scania 142 6x4 CHS 9X and then by the similar 142 D525 MHS. Bobby Martin usually drove this latter vehicle, which worked the length and breadth of the UK. When the M74 motorway was being built – down towards England – the WH Malcolm Scania and Foden 6x4s moved a huge number of 40-50 ton concrete beams, which were around 80-90' in length. A pair of independent bogies was also well used especially when Malcolms were moving some 110' long steel piles that came into Ardrossan by barge. But perhaps the most memorable work was done when Malcolms moved all the heavy equipment & drilling machines for the Howden Engineering concern. These were used in the construction of the Channel Tunnel and due to their size had to be shipped – from the Clyde to the English south coast – by barge, which was loaded (and unloaded) by the Malcolm crews.

Seen about 1991 are three generations of the Malcolm family - Donald, Andrew and Euan.

CHAPTER 10

Donald's Last Fight

Perhaps the biggest problem encountered by anyone who ever worked for Donald Malcolm for a long period of time, was the difficulty of trying to retire. In many respects, Donald was a lover of continuity and once he'd surrounded himself with a team he could rely on and trust, then he didn't want that to change – ever.

Part of Jack Love's work as Managing Director at WH Malcolm Ltd had been to enhance the original management pension scheme (which Grampian Holdings had created) to embrace all the Malcolm staff. And as time passed by, this Grampian pension was amended to allow staff members the option to take early retirement after they had reached 60 – provided they had at least 25 years service.

When you've worked under the pressure cooker of Malcolms for many years, such an option was considered to be very worthwhile. Many people thought it would be a good age to stop and still have time to be able to enjoy their retirement – but that was until Donald got to work on his psychological incentive scheme. 'Why don't you stay on a bit longer,' was perhaps his opening gambit and if that failed, he'd try: 'Go part time – just a few hours a day. You know you'll enjoy it. It'll give you something to occupy your time. You do a good job here – you know we don't want you to leave.' The persuasive chat just went on and on.

As mentioned earlier, Jack Love was drawn into this subtle agreement and he stayed on – in a variety of part time guises – until the age of 80. Many others have stayed in one form or another but some – like Peter Strachan and Tom Hamilton - who have insisted on retiring have been told that if they want to go, then they will have to find someone suitable to take their job – before they leave.

When Hughie Hastie wanted to take advantage of the early retirement offer, Donald's approach was entirely different as he just seemed to ignore what Hughie was saying: 'I was in charge of Murray Street stores then,' said Hughie, 'and I think Donald was happy with the job I was doing. But when the chance came to take early retirement, I gave Donald a year's notice that I was going to finish. He asked me to stay on but I said I'd had enough and I thought it was sorted. But actually all Donald did was lock out what I kept on saying to him. I kept telling him when I was finishing and he kept ignoring me. Even on the Friday night of my last day, I had a small drink with the lads downstairs and the last thing that Donald said to me then was: "See you on Monday, Hughie." He just didn't want me to go.'

The Big Man himself never had any qualms about how long he wanted to live and consequently, spend at work – his life was his job, the two were almost impossible to separate. 'I remember there was a few of us having a discussion about life,' recalled Donald's life long friend Cochrane McLeod. 'And I think it was my wife who commented that as you must get gradually infirm, surely no one would wish to live until they were 100. At that point, I remember Donald shooting his hand up and saying: "I do." His zest for life – and work - was always tremendous.'

IT STARTED WITH A SPOT

Like many major problems, Donald's battle with cancer started rather innocuously: 'Donald was complaining about some discomfort with his tongue,' recalled Wilma, 'and it was our daughter Wilma who looked at it. She said she could see a strange looking white spot and she told him he should go and see the doctor.'

It was in November 1986 when Donald first went to Canniesburn Hospital in Bearsden. Because of his expertise in oral cancer, Donald

93

Although the registrations from these MAN tippers suggest they were second hand buys, they did in fact come new but were sourced through an English based dealer. F561 CCT (plus 562 and 563) were three similar scow end dumpers, that could virtually take everything in their stride. Malcolms used this trio for all sorts of hard work and are particularly recalled as being used on sea defence work on places down the Ayrshire coast like Wemyss Bay. Perhaps their only drawback being their rear barn doors could prove difficult to open when twisted. The body fitted to the eight-wheel tipper F73 DDO allowed for a variety of traffic. MAN eight wheelers were bought in big numbers at the end of the 1980s and generally they did a very good job for Malcolms. However, the four bought with 5 cylinder engines, are recalled as being prone to crankshaft failure.

was referred to David Soutar who was a Consultant Plastic Surgeon and Head & Neck Surgeon. Following a biopsy of the white patch on his tongue, it showed evidence of a squamous (scaly or plate like) cell cancer. To say the news was devastating for the Malcolm family was putting it mildly: 'I'm sure we were told then that my Dad might only live for six months,' recalls his son Andrew, 'and even if the operation was a success, then there was a possibility that he might not be able to speak again.'

The operation went ahead and when it was finished, it was with a huge degree of trepidation that Andrew poked his head round the hospital bedroom door wondering whether his father was lying asleep or not. 'I heard this voice coming from the bed say, "Sit your f***ing self down," and it was probably the sweetest few words I've ever heard my Dad speak.'

That first operation (which saw the cancerous growth cut out) was a huge success but – understandably – the Malcolm family initially kept the news of Donald's condition fairly quiet. In truth, it was no big secret – as plenty people knew that Donald had been into hospital – although the recovery was remarkable. Even when Jack Semple interviewed Donald at length in July 1987 (for a feature in Truck Magazine) the journalist had no idea of anything untoward: 'Donald seemed perfectly normal and vibrant to me,' said Jack who recalls the energy in which he put into virtually everything – including the interview. 'I remember there was a pile of freshly arrived post on his desk and he just seemed to devour it in seconds. He came across as being a compulsive manager with a superb eye on the detail that could turn a profit. "The extra job that a lorry does in the afternoon makes all the difference with profitability," he told me. And even the way he talked on the phone was both clipped and decisive. He always seemed to end a conversation with the words: "Thank you, bye." But the way he said it so quickly, meant it came out like one word. It was more like a command – albeit a pleasant one – as well as a valediction. It was obvious that he was certainly a canny operator.'

BACK TO CANNIESBURN

Getting back into the routine after his first operation was a sheer pleasure for Donald as the WH Malcolm business was his life. And for the next five years, things went as routinely as they

could although by then he had given up cigar smoking. Every day without any untoward symptoms occurring was another sign that the cancer had gone away completely but in 1991 it recurred – in the same place. David Soutar and the Canniesburn team carried out further surgery and although signs looked well to start with, the tumour recurred in his tongue during 1993. On this occasion, the Consultant felt that even more surgery would be too debilitating: 'It would have required removal of too much of the tongue for him to function properly and we elected to give him radiotherapy,' recalled David Soutar.

Despite this aggressive treatment, the tumour recurred in 1995 and he underwent interstitial brachytherapy - a specialised technique, which sees high doses of radiotherapy applied to the tongue. This was followed by courses of chemotherapy.

It's virtually impossible to imagine the pain and anguish which Donald suffered in the latter part of his life. We can all imagine how harsh a simple toothache can seem but the amount of oral surgery that Donald underwent just beggar's belief: 'I think in the 18 years or so he received treatment,' recalled his wife Wilma, 'he underwent something like 18 major operations.'

Why the cancer kept coming – and going – over such a long period of time remained a mystery, even to David Soutar: 'It's highly unusual for a residual and recurring tumour to keep re-appearing with monotonous regularity,' he said. 'I sometimes felt that Donald frightened the cancer off – in the same way that Donald's awesome presence used to frighten some people. He certainly showed great resolve – as did his family.'

Donald had a pragmatic approach as the hospital staff reckoned he was determined to fight as long as possible – and as hard as possible - to see both his children and grandchildren grow up, as much as possible. 'I think in all the time my Dad underwent treatment,' recalled his son Walter, 'I only ever saw him once drop his head in anguish. The hospital tried a new form of treatment and when it didn't fully succeed, my Dad took it badly. I think I said, "The hospital aren't giving up on you, so you aren't going to, are you?" and of course he didn't.'

One major progressive consequence of having so many operations on his tongue and mouth area was that Donald was unable to eat – or even drink any form of hot fluids - as much as he once did. Consequently, combined with the multiple operations, radiotherapy & chemotherapy, he lost a huge amount of weight. His passion for being involved with the WH Malcolm business didn't waver however, so in the early days – at least – Donald almost ordered David Soutar and the Canniesburn team to do whatever they had to do, as quickly as possible: 'I don't think he ever discharged himself,' recalled the Consultant, 'but he certainly made it clear that he only wanted to stay one night – whatever we were doing.' Donald made it clear that so far as priorities were concerned, his involvement in the running of the WH Malcolm business was his – first - major concern.

The development of mobile phones was of course an obvious lifeline (to keep Donald in touch with base) but of course these were forbidden in hospital as their signals could affect all manner of equipment. This didn't stop Donald regularly having a phone smuggled into the hospital and because the staff got upset if he openly used it, Donald would perhaps creep into the toilet and conduct his calls while flushing the cistern. To Donald, keeping in touch with everyone at work was simply considered to be as good a therapy as medication.

CHANGES WITH GRAMPIAN

At the same time as Donald was requiring so much medical attention, the fortunes of Grampian Holdings PLC were also fluctuating. Grampian was probably at its peak at the start of the 1990s when it had something like 116 million shares in issue. Its four main areas of expertise were in Animal Pharmaceuticals, Sporting Goods, Woollen Goods and Road Transport and in 1990, these divisions generated a turnover of £140 million with pre-tax profit being £13.1 million.

Donald Slattery's expertise with his crane wagon earned him the nickname: 'King of the Hiabs.' Actually the Foden eight wheeler F430 DHS had a rear mounted Atlas of Blackwood crane which Donald got new: 'The first job it did was down in England and Donald Malcolm was so keen to get it working that he sent me down before the Foden was painted.' Reckoned to be one of the busiest motors on the fleet, Donald reckoned he slept more nights in the cab than he did at home. Loading port-a-cabins onto other vehicles was a regular job but most prestigious load for Donald and his Foden was when he lifted the Paisley Loom. This very expensive piece of sculptured steel was later taken to a show in England (by another vehicle) and then disappeared: 'No one knows where it went – and I think it cost Paisley Council about £60,000.'

In 1991, things didn't exactly go to plan when a protracted £60 million bid to acquire the healthcare group Macarthy PLC was lost to Lloyds Chemists. In 1993, it was decided to sell the Woollen Goods Retail division to the Edinburgh Woollen Mill (in exchange for the issue of a 25% share in that company) however within three years Grampian decided to buy the remaining 75% of EWM - and 100% of their principal supplier, Scottish Woollens Group.

In 1997, Grampian posted record profits of £13.71 million however this was on a turnover of £203.72 million. Grampian Pharmaceuticals was sold off in that year – for £67.8 million – and over the next three years the Sporting Goods portfolio was also gradually sold off. The feeling from the City of London (from Institutional shareholders and corporate advisors) was that huge conglomerates with so many diverse interests like Grampian were no longer fashionable.

By the start of the New Millennium, Grampian found themselves owning two very large players – in two entirely different domains. The Board had to decide which of either the Malcolm Group or Edinburgh Woollen Mill had the most development potential so about 2001, EWM was sold off to Venture Capitalists. And – as a natural progression – with the Malcolm Group then being the only asset of Grampian Holdings PLC, there was a degree of logic to change the Grampian name to that of The Malcolm Group PLC.

Donald's failing health meant he took no part in these last few years of decision-making. After enjoying a big family gathering to mark his 70th birthday (in 1995) he decided to step down from the Grampian board in 1996 when his place was taken by his son Andrew.

The following few years of treatment (combined with Donald's maturing years) was to be particularly demanding. In March 2001 he developed a further recurrence and underwent surgery followed by a further course of

After the Scania 142 6x4 D525 MHS finished its low loading duties, it was converted for recovery work. Fitted with Boniface Interstate recovery equipment, 'The Beast' was also given the personalised registration of WHM 540 to disguise the fact it's now approaching 20 years old. Being low geared – for heavy haulage work – it's only capable of 49-50mph. Of all the current South Street garage staff who drives the vehicle, Phil Conner is the one who thinks the most of it.

As well as maximum weight artics, tippers and low loaders, WH Malcolm have always had a modest requirement for smaller size, local distribution vehicles as shown in this Andrew Burton photograph of D678 NUS. However, in endeavouring to get the best of both worlds from this section of the fleet, Andrew Malcolm converted an eight wheel MAN tipper chassis – G84 MHS – into a full-length curtainsider. 'I wanted a distribution vehicle which could also bring back loads of glass into our Burnbrae Road warehousing. An eight-wheeler chassis gave us the capacity in respect of both height and weight while it also gave us the peace of mind of stability.' With the MAN proving the idea, Andrew then bought the eight wheel Volvo FL7 M514 BHS in April 1995 specifically with curtainsider bodywork in mind. 'That one had a fold down bunk in the cab,' said Andrew Malcolm, 'but to tell you the truth, it wasn't that comfortable to sleep in.' Again pictured by Andrew Burton, this long serving eight-wheeler is seen at Hellifield on the edge of the Yorkshire Dales National Park.

chemotherapy. Within a year, however, he was found to have a residual tumour in his tongue and jaw. By June 2002, the team at Canniesburn realised they had exhausted all their cancer treatments and all that was left was to look after his pain & control his symptoms.

While all this was going on, Donald always found great pleasure in being able to drive himself, wherever he had the inclination to go. His destinations were generally closer to home but the registration number UHS 1 became a regular sight in the area. Perhaps some would say Donald should have stopped driving long before he did, but the family knew that being his own driver was one thing which Donald really loved. Even after his first heart attack – in 2001 – he kept going although by the start of 2003, even he knew that his driving days were up.

END OF AN ERA

Speak to anyone who came into contact with Donald Malcolm for any length of time and you can rest assured that they would recall the sheer aura & presence of the man. That strength of character is reflected in how long & hard he fought against the medical problems he endured over 18 years.

This was a man who loved to eat, smoke cigars and enjoy a drink of brandy on a night, but these simple pleasures were taken away from him for many years. Towards the end, any sustenance that Donald received had to be liquidised and fed to him through a tube. Just imagine how that must feel by someone who simply loved the taste of a steak fillet between his teeth.

Donald was a man who loved to talk to (or perhaps shout at) people and he would never let any of his family or staff pass-by without a chat. But as a result of the never-ending succession of operations, even having a simple conversation grew harder by the day. Close friends and family would perhaps understand what he was trying to utter but to someone who ran his life & business through chatting on the phone, try and imagine what it's like when you can't even do that.

Donald simply absorbed everything which life threw at him and while many of a lesser stature

At the start of the 1990s, WH Malcolm had around nine Hino tippers in service. F370, 371 and 380 DHS also being recorded as three of them. All (apart from their first – a six wheeler) were eight wheel rigids and all are recalled with mixed feelings by Gordon Lawns, who is now Manager at South Street: 'I think all their drivers liked them because they were nice and comfortable to drive. But they had a big, non-turbo engine and they were absolutely gutless. They were very reliable but when we wanted back-up for them, that was a bit slow.' In early 2006, Malcolms were taking delivery of 10 Hino new eight wheelers: 'They're an entirely different motor,' promises Gordon.

A walk round any of the Malcolm Construction Services yards will reveal all manner of diverse – and very specialised – equipment. The 830 Trommel (top) is a specialised grading machine built by Powerscreen of Ireland. With a price tag of £103,000 mark (and a rolling weight of about 25 tonnes) the self-contained unit can grade – and separate – all manner of material on site.

The loading shovel (centre) is a Volvo L150C and is capable of lifting 10 tonnes. The large bucket has special hardened steel tips (or teeth) which can vary in manufacture depending on the material they are picking up. These tips are replaceable depending on how quickly they wear out.

MJ 997 is one of the four or five JCB 7 tonners, the company used. Close examination of this machine reveals an off set boom. Most crawler machines like this, which slew, generally have to work at an angle to themselves. But the JCB can pivot its boom so it can work parallel to itself – a huge asset when working in close confines.

would have buckled – and perhaps given up with life – this was one unique individual who simply got on with it. True he had the satisfaction of knowing that with his sons Andrew and Walter at the helm, the Malcolm Group was in very safe hands and even in the darkest hours, there were odd moments of light relief. While some of the best laughs Donald got was with a simple lapel type badge: 'I think it was Alan Bowes who saw it and brought it back from holiday,' recalled Donald's wife Wilma. 'But whenever someone was getting too frustrating for Donald to deal with, he'd simply push it into their face and get his message across.'

The writing on the badge was short – and to the point: 'What part of "f**k off" don't you understand,' it read – without having the two offending letters removed. To someone who was blunt, direct, not even the slightest bit politically correct and enduring all manner of hellish pain, anguish & frustration, this tiny bit of plastic was a small way of showing his true backbone.

There comes an end for all of us and for Donald it came swiftly: 'It was on the Saturday morning and Donald hadn't been up too long when I heard him collapse in the room next door,' recalled Wilma. Fortunately, Wilma's long-term companion and friend of the family, Helen Willock was there to give Donald a hand. 'Kitchen,' was apparently the only word he was able to say but Helen was able to help him take his normal seat in the family kitchen next to his wife and he died – quite quickly – as the pair were holding hands: 'I think he'd been ready to die for some time,' said Wilma as to the mixed emotions that she felt on his passing. Sorrow, of course, was felt but all of the family were bound to feel some relief – as to the end of his suffering - on Donald's behalf.

The funeral was held on Friday 9th May but for friends and close family, the intervening time was probably the longest week of their lives. Donald's body was embalmed and placed in an open coffin at Boghouse where he was seen – and spoken to – by family, friends & many members of staff. And after such a solemn occasion as this, many of those came out of the room with a smile on their face: 'Donald was dressed in a suit,' said Wilma, 'but I think it was Andrew who pinned his "f**k off" badge to his lapel. Everyone who saw it seemed to think it just suited the occasion fine.'

There weren't many smiles amongst the thousands of mourners who subsequently gathered at Houston & Killellan Church when Rev. Georgie Baxendale conducted the funeral service. And perhaps the expressions on all those who were listening would certainly have changed when she began by saying: 'Donald Malcolm was a terrible, terrible man.' Donald would have loved the approach she took because it caught people's attention to hear her follow by saying: 'Terribly good, terribly kind.'

Donald Malcolm was a lot of things to a lot of people. He was a husband, a father, a brother and a son. He was also 'The Boss' and he was also The Big C – in one of the many jokes that was told against him – and by him (to hear the joke, just ask any of the old Malcolm salts – they all know it and still laugh at it).

He was also a friend and an unassuming saviour – to many people. He could – apparently – have been awarded something like an OBE but when discreet approaches were made from the relevant authorities, Donald made it clear he wasn't interested in any form of recognition like that – the fortunes of his family and The Malcolm Group were the only recognition he strove for. He also did a lot (without making any fuss) which even the family didn't know about: 'It was only after the funeral,' said Wilma, 'that people came up and told me some of the things which Donald had either paid for or done and we were all totally unaware of it.'

The local church, however, was aware of the huge donations he made while David Soutar recalled the annual – significant – donations, which Donald made to the Canniesburn Research Trust, for further research into oral cancer.

Donald's body was laid to rest in the new part of Houston cemetery while also in the coffin (as well as that certain lapel badge) was his infamous little black book. Those involved in carrying his body – and attending to the procedure at the graveside – were Walter & Andrew Malcolm, Walter's son Donald - named after his grandfather – Ian Mitchell (a cousin) Gordon White & Adrian Scott (sons in law) and Martin Kiely & George Scott, who were both employees of the company. This was not the most pleasant of tasks they were to ever perform, but if they hadn't want to do it, the fact that there would have been hundreds of volunteers to take their place reflects on how Donald Malcolm was regarded.

And one more thing, don't think this is the end of the Donald Malcolm story.

Malcolm Plant operated three Foden low loader tractor units in the late 1980s / early '90s, two 6x4s and the sole 4x2 – F426 DHS. Although only used in Category 1 of the Special Types General Order (which gave a limit of 46 tonnes gross), the 4400 tractor proved versatile enough to couple to standard 40' trailers when required. Jim Anderson recalls the pictured step frame, semi-trailer also proved very versatile and had a 25 tonnes capacity. It's seen carrying a Tulloch Construction Telehandler, fitted with a front-loading bucket.

The Kilwinning based S427 HGD was pictured by Brian McGinley in Kincardine, Fife during April 2001. The Volvo FL10 360 tractor unit was amongst the last of this model (before the FM12 replaced it) and generally felt to be down on power when fully loaded. Regular loads of coal were hauled from Killoch near Coylton to Longannet power station, with fly ash being the ideal back load. As the rather special front tow hitch suggests, some of the Ayrshire based Malcolm tippers went into all sorts of strange sites. In order that they could be towed out without causing any damage, the Volvo factory at Irvine worked closely with Malcolms to re-design the front tow brackets. Winston Wright, the Volvo factory manager, in particular being recalled as instrumental with the new engineering.

In 1999, the 35 strong fleet of the Blackburn based Wilfred Holden was acquired. The type of operation which Holden were involved in at the time was compatible with the Malcolm workload and with Holdens wishing to sell, the transaction proved to be a natural fit. The Holden fleet at that time was 100% ERF and although then about 15 years old, the ERF 'B' Series B376 YCW was given a fresh coat of Malcolm paint and worked as a shunter.

Dan Eadie is the pictured WH Malcolm driver seen supervising the unloading of his Renault Kerax at Hillington in October 2004. Dan joined WH Malcolm in 1991 and drove their first eight-wheel curtainsider G84 MHS: 'I really liked that old motor,' said Dan, 'and in truth it seemed to go better when it had 18 tonnes of Iron Bru on its back. I'd have been quiet happy to have kept it but it was sold in 2001.' The pictured Kerax was also delivered new - in September 2002 - as a tipper chassis but converted in house, for curtainsider use. It did its first 18 months service based at customer's premises in Barrow upon Soar in Leicestershire. Following a change of operational requirements – rather poignantly - this Kerax was later converted back into a tipper and became the only tipper at Malcolms painted in their blue livery. It was sold in that guise during April 2006.

Including their courtship, Donald and Wilma were to spend something like 53 years together.

The Legacy

The transition from one generation to the next, in any form of family business, doesn't always come easily. When Donald Malcolm's father died – suddenly – it was fortunate that Marion Malcolm had the support and determination to keep the business going at the same time as raising her young family. Although, it's reasonable to infer that she always anticipated her son Donald taking over the business reins as soon as he was old enough.

However, close to 70 years later, when Donald's health was failing, the family no longer owned the WH Malcolm business. And the PLC board (in theory) could well have head hunted someone suitable – outside the business & family - to take control. Again, if you believe that, then you'll believe anything because as long as Donald Malcolm had a breath in his body, then he would never have allowed anyone but a Malcolm to take over 'his' transport group. In fairness, it would have been very difficult for the PLC board to even consider such a move as Donald's two sons – Andrew & Walter – would never have worked under anyone else. As was said right at the outset of this story, the WH Malcolm business is unique. In many respects, the evolvement of the Malcolm family – the two boys especially – was something like a breed of lion cubs growing up. When they were very young, they may have played together and enjoyed the multitude of sights on display in the big world around them, but they would never have thought of testing the dominant male family head. They always looked to that experienced leader for guidance, but as soon as they developed their own particular strengths & thoughts, they eventually felt it was time to establish their own mark on how their life should evolve - even though those thoughts may be totally alien to what the family head decreed.

With Donald & Wilma having four children, it was to be expected the makeup of their family would be a mix of their parent's genes: 'My daughter Wilma and my youngest Andrew both take after Donald,' laughs their mother Wilma, 'as they can have a lot of fire to their nature. Although both Marion and Walter seem to have a quieter disposition - they take after me.'

In many respects, Donald always loved having his four children (and any of their friends) around their Boghouse home and Wilma recalls how empty he felt the place was (in the mid 1980s) when they all eventually moved out. This didn't mean everything was sweetness and light in the Malcolm household: 'Donald would never swear in front of the children when they were young,' says Wilma, 'but the arguments about business – especially with Andrew – when they were older, turned the air blue.' And Wilma can testify how those disagreements also tested the strength of the door hinges and the glass panels throughout the Malcolm home.

IMAGE

In his heart of hearts, Donald Malcolm was always a tipper man. And while he'd be the first to admit that the huge growth of the Malcolm Group was to eventually come through the general haulage side of affairs (Logistics Division as the integration of the work is now known) to Donald, the flats – and curtainsiders - were always a poor relation to his beloved tippers.

It was perhaps an ideal situation that the WH Malcolm business had these two entirely different aspects. After Andrew learnt the ropes driving a variety of trucks, his passage – via the traffic desk – into administration saw him naturally drift towards general haulage. And when Tom Hamilton was eventually allowed to fully retire in 1988, Andrew was to be given his head – with the long distance work – having Charles Stewart and the rest of the Malcolm management team to look after him.

The WH Malcolm depot at Gatenby in North Yorkshire was just about to be added to the Malcolm portfolio, while the following 18 years was to see a massive expansion of the Malcolm Logistics network. The period also saw a move round of the Malcolm administrative staff. At the end of the 1980s, HQ for Logistics became freshly built office premises on the Burnbrae Road site in Linwood although by 1997, they had moved again the short distance to the Company's current HQ in Burnbrae Drive. This is adjacent to the company's purpose built Maintenance Services Division. Seen from above, the premises in Burnbrae Road and Cartside are very close together and it wasn't long before Malcolms built their own piece of road to join them up and so take away a huge amount of through traffic from the town of Johnstone.

Andrew's elder brother Walter was to follow his father onto the tipper side of the Malcolm business around 1982 (working from Murray Street in Paisley) after spending three years studying accountancy at the University of Strathclyde. This business method of training was to stand Walter in good stead but both the brothers say how much they learnt from their father: 'If you look after the pennies then the pounds will look after themselves,' was one of his many expressions which Walter recalls.

Donald's memory of facts, figures, registrations, names – and quirks – of virtually everyone and every vehicle he came into contact with is legendary. With his little black book (or rather assortment of books) being his own company bible of vehicles. Everyone was aware of his temper – with the rider 'His bark's worse than his bite' – and while Donald never bore a grudge, he always fought hard, especially to keep his own traffic: 'Never let the competition take away your work,' Walter recalls him saying. 'You have to fight hard to keep your customer satisfied.'

It was attempting to keep a potential customer happy that prompted Andrew Malcolm to take a huge decision: 'I was giving a presentation to a highly respected concern and was emphasising how well turned out our vehicles were,' says Andrew. 'However when the customer turned round and said he'd just seen one of our tippers which looked battered & filthy, I realised we'd have to make the difference – between the two divisions of Construction & Logistics – more apparent.'

The launch of that difference (about 1993) was to be a change of livery for the entire Construction Services Division. But to say the move was greeted with disdain – by Donald and virtually everyone else in the company – is putting it mildly: 'My brother in law, Gordon White, is a graphic designer and he'd come up with a new colour scheme of yellow, green and blue which we'd started using on all the plant machinery. When my Dad was away on holiday, I decided to repaint one of the blue tippers using this yellow based plant style of livery but he was furious when he first saw it.' Everyone seemed to be against the idea but Andrew stuck to his guns and although it took a while to be accepted, the die was cast and every tipper since, has been of the same distinctive – and refreshing - colours.

The adoption of Company uniforms was also a huge pill for Donald to swallow. To someone who was always concerned about the balance sheet performance, giving out shirts, trousers, jackets and the like to all the staff was simply eroding the bottom line of profitability: 'Send that stuff back,' was the printable version of Donald's shouted message to Alan Linklater when he first cast eyes on it.

But just like the change of tipper livery, the uniform has of course stayed. And while Donald may have huffed and chuffed and swore profusely – at all & sundry and Andrew in particular – about the changes that was going on, he had no one to blame but himself.

That may seem contradictory but it all boils down to Donald Malcolm's legacy. While a legacy is normally the material effects of someone's will, Donald also left a huge amount of intangibles to his successors – not least of which was the way the business should be run. To someone who was virtually his shadow, Andrew became indoctrinated into the Malcolm way of doing things from a very early age. And so far as he is concerned – even now - that's the only way things can be done.

END OF THE PLC

From being a relatively huge conglomerate in its Grampian days, The Malcolm Group PLC became a fairly small concern with around 65 million shares. Although turnover was growing dramatically, the increase in insurance premiums (following the 9/11 terrorist incident) together with rises in fuel & wage costs linked to the implications of the Working Time Directive combined to squeeze the PLC's profitability. The relevant figures posted for the 2003 accounts were a profit of £7.4 million on a turnover of £129.1 million.

It quickly became apparent that some shareholders wanted better returns and it was suggested The Malcolm Group should be sold. As soon as the word was put out, there was naturally a huge amount of interest in taking on such a successful enterprise. However the sheer makeup of the Malcolm Group was in itself off putting.

There was interest from Logistics concerns but they didn't want to buy the localised Construction Services division. Conversely, those parties interested in taking on the tippers & plant side of Malcolms had no wish to acquire a fleet of curtainsiders or a far flung depot / warehousing network. Walter Malcolm summed the quandary of many would be bidders by saying: 'They all said that the Malcolm Group just couldn't work in theory. But of course in practice, we did work – and we worked very well.'

With overtures for the Group coming from two different directions, there was a possibility that the PLC could hive off the two divisions so they could be sold separately. Such a thought was unthinkable to the family because they knew it was the entire WH Malcolm management team, which made the company work. So who were better suited to lead a buy out bid than the Malcolm brothers – Andrew and Walter. That bid was finalised in May 2005 when the brothers – and their backers – acquired the relevant numbers of shares and so brought the Malcolm Group back into private hands.

A CONTINUING STORY

Donald Malcolm wasn't around to see that huge step back into family ownership. But those who knew him will probably tell you he would have had a huge grin of satisfaction in how things have evolved.

The evolution of his beloved tippers took another step forward in 2005 when the new South Street 'super depot' was opened. This allowed for the closure of the smaller tipper depots around Glasgow (including the old tipper HQ at Murray Street) although tippers are still operated independently at Kilwinning. Malcolm Plant Ltd is also now based in South Street it being the last Malcolm company to leave Brookfield (in 1997) when it was then re-located to Murray Street.

The structure of how the Malcolm tippers now work was to change following the introduction of the Land Fill Tax in 1996. What Peter Strachan started doing (in the late 1960s) at Donald's suggestion of offering a Malcolm package of manpower, tipping vehicles, plant & machinery – plus expertise – was taken on and enthusiastically developed by Martin Kiely. This total package formulae, has now become standard practice for the majority of work carried out by the Construction Services Division.

From February 2000, the Malcolm Logistics Services was to include an express rail freight operation which saw a scheduled service between Aberdeen, Grangemouth, Mossend, Linwood and Crick (which is part of the Daventry International Rail Freight Terminal). In the 21st century, more road hauliers are realising that utilising the railway network is good business sense and WH Malcolm has saved a huge amount of road going mileage by using rail. During 2005, in excess of 20 million road miles were saved by the Malcolm road going fleet – by putting their loads onto the train. However, as early as the 1960s, Donald Malcolm was moving blaes – in bulk - by rail from Livingston to Glasgow and so cut down on his road fleet's mileage, which just illustrates how far sighted Donald was.

Networking with British Industry is how Malcolm Logistics now offers itself to its customer base through their chain of strategically placed UK depots. Malcolm's long-standing relationship with many leading national and international companies has evolved into the type of integrated service their individual customers require. Yet also able to change, whenever the need is required.

Things have come a long way since Donald Malcolm first came into the world in 1925. But even though he may have died in 2003, don't think – again - this is the end of the Donald Malcolm story. True, it may be the end of this particular appreciation of his life, but the way he conducted himself and the influence he had on so many people into them being 'Malcolmised', means that effect is set to run on for the foreseeable future.

When you look at their big hands – or even the shape of their shoulders – or a multitude of their personal mannerisms, the genetic inheritance from Donald Malcolm is still very much on show in his two sons Andrew and Walter. And you don't have to study too closely the demeanour of Andrew's eldest son Euan to see he's almost a carbon copy of what his father was like when he was growing up as Donald's shadow.

But really you should forget about the Malcolm family because it's natural they are bound to inherit the Malcolm way of doing things. Instead, look at the many people, whom Donald came into contact with. It's their 'Malcolmised' way of doing things, which is Donald Malcolm's biggest legacy. How they run their own life – and the influence they have on many others – is down to Donald's way of doing things.

If you think that's hard to believe, then speak to anyone who had dealings with him. In many respects, unique may be too mild a word to describe the life & times – and persona - that was Donald Malcolm.

The Malcolm family gathered together in 1995 to celebrate Donald's 70th birthday. The back row – from left to right – are: Gordon White with his arm supporting Malcolm White; Andrew Malcolm holding Ker Malcolm; Fiona Malcolm; Walter Malcolm holding James Malcolm; Yvonne Malcolm. In the centre row - from left to right – are: Marion White holding Caitlin White (but also pregnant with Ben White); Donald Malcolm junior; Donald holding Euan Malcolm; Wilma Malcolm; Wilma Scott holding Lara Scott (and Wilma too was pregnant with Thomas Scott); Adrian Scott. In the front row – left to right – are: Eva Scott; Nicola Malcolm; Clare Malcolm and Rachel Malcolm. The inserts show – in later years – Ben White and Tom Scott – plus the Scott dog, Angel.

I remember Donald

Steve Bryant who now heads up Scot JCB has been supplying the Malcolm Group with JCB machines since 1978. 'Donald was a ruthlessly astute negotiator, who had the uncanny knack of being able to squccze the last few pounds out of a supplier but always with charm and humour. His little black book in which he wrote every lorry and item of plant he had purchased and its price was always referred to in negotiations. I can remember one meeting before Christmas when talks had commenced at 5pm and by 7.15pm a deal was agreed. I looked at my watch and Donald realised that I had a problem; I was due to look after the children at 7.30pm. Immediately Donald phoned my wife and stated that it was his fault I was going to be late and he then turned to me and said: "Take one of the hampers as a peace offering to your wife." These were the actions of a man who understood the importance of a happy family life. It was always a pleasure dealing with Donald and having met him first when I was a young man, he was a great example to me of how to conduct business with honesty, integrity and great enthusiasm and all this in the tough world of construction plant hire and road haulage.'

Margaret Connell worked in the Admin office at Murray Street for 28 years from 1970. 'My main memory of Donald was in how he was a very fair person and if he could do you a good turn, then he would do it. Yes, he was outspoken and his language – to some – was very choice, but he didn't use it with me. Although I always told him he had a degree in French – because of his use of the f word. He was a great believer of the family idea and if a member of staff wanted to bring their son – or daughter – into the Malcolm business, then Donald would always try and help to accommodate them. I suppose the reason why people worked hard for him was they all knew he was a workaholic.'

George Cunningham's father – who was also called George – ran G&D Cunningham at Galston in Ayrshire. Although in competition with WH Malcolm in some respects, George recalls the two companies worked closely together on fly ash work while the two families also socialised together. 'Like many people,' said George, 'I've lots of thoughts & memories about Donald but there's some you can't print. I remember not too long before the end going to see him and how he insisted on giving us the guided tour. He was so proud of how his two sons had developed the Malcolm Group. Donald had a fearful reputation and I fell out with him regularly. He worked hard to keep his own customers, as he didn't like people coming into his area to compete with him. But once he became your friend, you were a friend for life and I'll never forget how helpful he was to me when my father died.'

Fred Davie was Commercial Director at Redfearn Glass in Barnsley and made use of Malcolm's transport & warehousing facilities to handle his company's product from 1979. 'I always had a lot of respect for Donald as he was someone you could always trust – he called a spade, a spade. He said to me he'd never lost a customer and you always knew where you stood with him. He had a great sense of humour but kept his finger very much on the pulse. I honestly feel he was one of the last true characters of the transport industry.'

Mae Innes was Donald's secretary at Murray Street for 28 years before retiring in 1994. 'He was a good boss to work for and I quite enjoyed my time there. I remember how he had a tremendous memory and he also had the ability to hang onto his key members of staff. It was having people around him - like the Financial Director Hugh Stevenson - who proved how important the whole Malcolm management team was to the company's success. Donald may have had quite a bark but if anyone was in need of help, he was always the first person to stretch out a helping hand.'

Martin Kiely is Managing Director of the Malcolm Group's Construction Services Division. 'Like so many people in the construction industry, I dealt with Donald and his company all my working life yet it wasn't until I worked for him that I got to know the real man. Here was an old man, who had fought illness for so long and yet had drive, energy and an appetite for his business like I had never seen before. He was simply awesome. Donald also had the most wicked sense of humour and a temper to match – and always found time for both no matter how busy we were! People have told stories of Donald in abundance, but there was another side to him. Donald loved people, especially those around him. He always had time for everyone and helped countless people in so many ways, but did it privately - he didn't like his caring soft side to become too public. There was nothing better when you had a problem or were under pressure, Donald would sit down with you for a cup of tea (he loved his tea) and talk things through. He didn't always have the answers for you, but you left feeling great and ready to take on the world. Above all, Donald's greatest motivation to succeed was his family - family meant everything to Donald and in his eyes, I'm sure, his family would be his greatest achievement. Over the few years I knew him, Donald became a real father figure to me and - I'm not ashamed to say - I loved him like a father. There are still too many days that I wish my door would open and he would come in for that cup of tea.

Derek Leggate is Managing Director of Volvo Truck & Bus, Scotland. 'Although I joined the company in 1981, I only began dealing with Donald – on the truck selling side - in 1990. To say that I was very green – in that respect - is something of an understatement, but Donald took me through the learning curve. Yes, he pushed hard on the deal but he knew when to stop and I have a lot to thank him for - he taught me a lot.'

Freddie McAllister is Fleet Engineer at Malcolm's Construction Services. He started with the company at Murray Street in 1970 while his father – Wullie – also did 30 years at Malcolms. 'Donald was quite a character. He was brilliant in

the way he could always seem to get the best out of anyone. He was a hard worker with a good sense of humour and he was fair. I remember him saying: "You don't spend anything, you couldn't afford," so he was very guarded with expenditure. He also seemed to know everything you didn't and he also had the habit of popping up anywhere. He was a rough diamond – I liked him.'

Charlie Mair joined Malcolm Plant Ltd about 1966 and became a Director during his 35 years service there. 'Donald was a very fair man and his word, was his bond. Mind he wanted his pound of flesh, as he was a hard, hard, hard man to work for. But saying that, the job itself was good and I enjoyed working for him. He had a great sense of humour and a huge personality. When he walked into the room, he had a terrific presence about himself.'

Andrew McGarva is a Project Director of Amec Group Ltd and first met Donald in 1995 when tenders for haulage were being sort for the new M77 motorway. 'I remember after we eventually shook hands on the deal how Donald said: "For a Sassenach, you drive a hard bargain," but I also remember how much he put into that very complex project. The new road was 11 kilometres long and fraught with problems but first thing on a morning – and last thing at night – you could guarantee that Donald would be on site ensuring all the Malcolm men & machines, were doing exactly what they had to as it was Donald's presence which kept everyone on their toes. And it was his commitment to that particular job which made it a success. I know he was suffering with medical problems at the time but his enthusiasm & drive just belied that condition – and his years. I'm sure he enjoyed being involved in such a complex project. It's something of a Malcolm trademark that their word is their bond – and that's the reason why we continue to use their services. But I'm sure that approach is a one which Donald created – I had a lot of time for him.'

David McGibbon was Finance Director of Grampian PLC and had close contact with Donald from 1977. 'The Grampian – Malcolm marriage was very successful because Donald's forte was the running of his business - and he did it very well. There are lots of things I remember about him. He had this habit of saying: "Mark my card." He always wanted to know what was going on and kept up-to-date and even if there was a problem, it was always best to put Donald in the picture than hope he'd never find out. To him, family was very important – and he always asked after them – but really, he used to reckon the whole workforce was his family. He was very protective of them – even though he could ball them out. He had a great sense of humour and a heart of gold and they truly threw away the mould after they made him. He was a larger than life character.'

John McKay became Section Manager at Ravenscraig steel works and used Malcolm's haulage fleet from 1977 until the plant closed in 1992. 'Donald was an outstanding person in the haulage industry and known by everyone. He cracked the whip with his workers but he was a dynamic, go-ahead person who chased every bit of business, which he thought he could do. He gathered a good bunch of directors round him and I remember how he worked very closely with us when pressures were on us to cut costs and be more efficient. To me – and my wife - he was a very good friend and I have some very, very fond memories of us all together. He'll be sadly missed.'

Willie McNab is managing director of the Northern Ireland based RJ Maxwell first had dealings with Donald in 1995 when they were discussing tipper rates to surface the M77 motorway. 'I soon realised that Donald was a great believer of saying exactly what he felt – no matter what it sounded like. When we first met, we couldn't agree on rates and even though Donald had asked us to stay for something to eat, his retort to what I suggested for payment was: 'Eat your roll, drink your tea and f**k off." But after that, we grew very close and to tell you the truth, I learnt a huge amount from Donald. You couldn't have dealings with the Big Man and not do so – in many respects, he was a mentor to me. His approach to business wasn't really on just getting the best price for the job in hand, he was really building foundations for jobs with you in the future. I also liked the story about the day when one of his drivers came into the Murray Street office and handed the clerk a small brown envelope for Donald. When she took it up to him, he opened it up and found a birth certificate. Donald went across to the window and shouted down to the driver: "What have you given me this for." To which the driver said: "It's just to prove I'm not a bastard." But even though Donald was suffering a bit with his speech, it didn't stop his enthusiasm for work. Our contract ran for 18 months and I was in our dispatch office one

Sunday afternoon and had to ring Malcolms wanting a few more trucks. And who should answer the phone but Donald – and he even got us the trucks we wanted. He always seemed to be there when you wanted him. If you had a problem – work or otherwise – Donald always did his best to help. I felt a great affinity towards him.'

Bobby Murie drove for WH Malcolm – on long distance work - for almost 37 years until he retired in 2000. 'Some people don't speak kindly about Donald but I wouldn't hear a bad word said against him. If you did your work he never bothered you and he would always remember if you did things to help him out – and he'd pay you well for what you did. I know he could shout at you or tear off a strip, but if he realised he was in the wrong, he'd be the first to apologise – and I admired him for that.'

Jimmy Paterson joined the company in 1964 and was to be the Manager at Kilwinning from 1967 until he retired in 2001. 'With my family's links into transport, I knew Donald from the age of 10. He always struck me as being a fair man who was a good communicator as he had the gift of being able to talk whatever the level of people he was addressing. We spoke on the phone at least twice a day and his main concern was if all the motors were out, as he trusted your judgement as to what was wanted. There's a couple of things I mostly remember about Donald – if you saw his left index finger crooked towards anyone then you knew they were in for a telling off. And I remember how he kept all his notes – and bits of paper – in his spectacle case but needed an elastic band round it to stop it bursting open.'

Alex Ross joined the huge engineering concern of Babcock in 1959 where he became Shipping Manager. He made great use of the WH Malcolm fleet throughout the 40 years he stayed with the company. 'Malcolms were a business who never let us down and that's why they became our predominant haulier. Donald tried very hard to give a good service and the excellent reliability of the company meant we considered them very professional. Even when we wanted something done in a hurry, we knew if we asked Malcolms then they would certainly do their best to help us out. I knew Donald very well socially and we had some really good times – with plenty laughs. He may have come across as a hard man but – when you got to know him – you found he had a soft centre.'

Peter Ross first began selling Scanias to Donald in the early 1980s when he was Managing Director of Reliable Vehicles Ltd. 'Donald was quite a character in lots of respects but always very astute. He liked a laugh and was as hard as it came but once you did the deal, the handshake meant everything. And there was never any quibble when you later went with an invoice as he paid there and then. He was very much a people person and liked to encourage fathers to bring their sons into the business. And he was a great believer of just dropping in for a mug of tea and a chat. I had plenty time for Donald especially after the way he fought against things at the end.'

George Scott is the Centre Manager of the Maintenance Services Division. Although he joined the company in 1974 (at the Russell Street, Johnstone depot) it wasn't until he moved to Linwood that he began seeing Donald on an almost daily basis. 'Donald was good to me and I think he enjoyed how I talked his talk. From about 1999 – when we began buying a lot of nearly new vans - we used to go to the auctions together and it was amazing how hundreds of folk used to come up to talk to him. Even when he was really ill, he loved to know what was going on. I admired him greatly as he was a good guy and a good employer. There'll never be another man like him.'

Billy Smith is now transport manager at Whiteinch Demolition but knew Donald personally for about 45 years. 'I suppose the main thing I remember about Donald was his photographic memory. It was unbelievable how much he could recall about vehicles or drivers he'd had from years back. He was a great guy who would tell you things straight to your face. He was very hard – in that he wanted 110% from his workers – but he was very fair. There'll never be anybody like Donald ever again – he was a great guy.'

John Smith used to run John Smith Contractors of Whiteinch. 'I suppose we were in the same line of work as Malcolms but Donald never tried to take any business off us. I always referred to him as "Mr Haulage" because although he had lots of staff, you knew he was always on top of the job. I don't know when Donald slept because he seemed to work round the clock. You have to give credit where it's due because Donald was a one off.'

George Walker retired in 2003 after clocking up around 30 years service with WH Malcolm. He finished as a Director – at Murray Street – but recalls working very closely with Donald for many years. 'Donald and I had the reputation of arguing together all the time but really it was just a bit of sport. And when I think back, he was good to me and I was good to him. Donald liked a good joke and one that did the rounds about his attitude to finances was about the day, when Donald went to Buckingham Palace to receive his Knighthood. After the Queen dubbed him on the shoulders with her sword, she said to him: "Arise, Sir Donald " but Donald didn't move. Again the Queen said: "Arise, Sir Donald," but again he didn't move. Then Prince Philip leaned over to the Queen and said: "You'll have to tell him to get up because he doesn't know what a rise means." He was very careful with the company's money but at the same time he was very generous in lots of respects – and he did a lot for charity, which no one knew anything about. He had a phenomenal memory but the main thing I remember was how hard he worked – he grafted harder than anybody else. I think that's why everyone worked so hard for him.'

Jack Wilkie joined Malcolms in 1965 and finished as Depot Manager at Murray Street when he retired 38 years later. 'Donald expected and got his pound of flesh as he was a hard taskmaster but he was very fair and there were a lot of good times – and always time for a bit of a laugh. Yes, we did argue but the next minute he'd be asking about your family – he cared a lot in that way. I always had great respect for Donald because of the way he treated me and there were a lot of good times over the years. He was a one off.'

Jim Yuill a fellow haulage contractor Yuill & Dodds, knew Donald for some 40 years. 'We worked very closely together with some tipper work over the years and although we were very close – socially – we could still fall out with each other. But a day wouldn't pass without us having a blether on the phone about this and that. I can remember arguing about rates with Donald and while he used to have his little black book, he scribbled any notes down on a bit of paper, I remember how he would pull his spectacle case out and keep the bits of paper in there. He could be a hard man at times but I suppose that's what kept him going towards the end – he didn't let his health problems hinder him. He was quite a character.'

I Remember Dad

Marion White says: 'It's so difficult to put into just a few words, my thoughts and feelings for a man like my Dad. There are so many stories to tell about him, he was such a great father and a great inspiration to me. Dad and I were always very close. Not only was I named after his beloved mum, but he always told me that I looked like her and had her cheeky sense of humour. I reckon I got away with an awful lot because of that! The flip side of being so close was that boyfriends were never very welcome as Dad never ever approved. He made things really quite difficult for them – I guess in his very direct way, he was testing them to see if they were good enough for me, poor souls! I remember bringing one unsuspecting boy home for a couple of hours. As we sat chatting, Dad announced: "Well son, goodnight." Being polite, the guy said: "Goodnight Mr Malcolm," expecting Dad to saunter off to bed. But that was definitely not Dad's plan – he came right back at the guy and replied: "No son you don't understand - when I go to bed, you f*** off!" Funnily, that relationship was short lived.

When I first met my husband, Gordon, a couple of weekends passed by and I hadn't been home for my usual visit. Then came the phone call. I was summoned to Brookfield and the interrogation began. When I admitted I had met someone I really liked, he said to mum: "I told you something was up Wilma," and then to me, "Who the hell is this boyfriend that's keeping you so busy and why haven't I met him?" I bravely replied: "Because I don't want this one scared off." Thankfully, he had the grace to laugh and Gordon was accepted into the family. Dad's attention to detail for the business is legendary but his attention to fashion much less so. Years ago, I bought him a funny tie emblazoned with MCP standing for Male Chauvinist Pig. He wore it for a month believing it actually said MPL for Malcolm Plant Limited. Glasses were soon ordered.

Dad and I shared a wicked sense of humour. Towards the end, when he was so very ill, I told him a story of when I had taken Ben, mine and Gordon's youngest son, to a dental hospital in a particularly rough area of Glasgow. I had gone straight from work in a smart suit and some particularly nice shoes I was very proud of, when a woman approached me. Looking me up and down, she said: "Can I ask you something, hen?" I thought she was going to ask me where I got my shoes but she said: "I know you - you drive the ice cream van in Easterhouse, don't you? I said to my daughter it's either her or she's got a double." That put me well in my place and when I told Dad, although he couldn't speak, he laughed and laughed at my shattered pride. I was really glad I could bring a bit of fun back into his life at a time when things were pretty bleak for him.

Throughout my married life, I saw Mum and Dad three or four times a week, and phoned absolutely everyday in life, no matter where in the world I was. Eventually, when he couldn't speak, a squeeze of the hand, a kiss blown, or his favourite affectionate waving of 2 fingers, was enough to know how much we both cared. He adored all his children and grandchildren, and as a cherished daughter it was so good to know how loved I was by both Mum and Dad, and it was a warm and lovely joy for me to give that love back in return. I can honestly say that I absolutely adored Dad. I also respected him enormously and I looked to him for advice on so many aspects of my life.

Dad very rarely called me Marion, it was always Mary-Anne. When he called me Marion, I knew I was in trouble. When he was angry or upset, Dad would always give a good rollicking but once it was over it was immediately forgotten. Like many daughters, when I was younger I got annoyed at how strict he was with me. Now as a mother, I appreciate and understand it, and I'm very grateful and happy that our children knew and loved him.

I am so proud to have been his daughter, he taught me so much. "Never get ideas above your station," he used to say, "because remember the people you meet on the way up are the same people you meet on the way down." I love, remember and miss him each and every day. I still seek his advice in my mind and can guess his reactions based on the many years he shaped and guided me. He was such a legend both as a father and as a businessman. I'm sure he's up there swearing for Scotland and shouting the odds at us all. He'll always be in our hearts and he can be proud that he was such a great influence on us all.'

Wilma Scott says: 'My earliest memories are of being with him in the car. Every Sunday he would take me to Auchans farm where his best friends, John and Janet Young, lived. I remember it was a real treat and a special time to be on my own with him.

On the way home we always stopped at Granny Malcolms' where I was always spoiled with treats and affection by granny and the two aunties who we always knew as Ag (Agnes) and Mog (Morag).

Dad hated holidays and over the years we learned to leave him alone for the first three days to help him acclimatise to relaxation. My mum used to furnish him with historical romantic novels, usually Scottish, and when you saw him in a deck chair with his shirt off, just simmet (vest) and braces reading his book, you knew he was beginning to wind down. He got a few bad sunburns from this practice.

On holiday in Blackpool once, we were in a hotel lift with music hall star Tessie O'Shea who had just written a diet book. She took one look at Dad and offered him a copy. He laughed and declined. He has always loved his food and had no vanity about his body.

We also met Sir Bill Shankly on that visit and Dad managed to get Walter his autograph.

Having lost his own Dad when he was only eight, Dad had no role model for parenthood. He loved us fiercely but adolescence and early adulthood were a foreign land in which he struggled to find a language. I in particular know that I pressed his buttons making career and life moves outside his experience and understanding. It hurt him deeply when I left home at 21, especially as he had done his best to thwart my leaving at 18 by not filling out the grant forms declaring the grant making body a nosy b———.

I don't think he was ever really comfortable with my absence from home, indeed from Scotland until I married as that was an acceptable reason for moving out.

In the early days of his cancer, he would phone me often. Walter's son, Donald had just been born and he was afraid and angry about the possibility of not seeing his grandchildren grow up. He found the confrontation with his mortality a very difficult one and the dance between his acceptance of it and denial, was one that continued into the very late stages of the awful parasitical illness that robbed him of his greatest pleasure; conversation and good food and best of all conversation and good food with people he loved. He had many, many friends and every Saturday night would be spent with a few of them over a meal or at one of the hundreds of weddings and dinner dances he and Mum attended over the years.

On my wedding day, the drive to the church, the walk down the aisle and his speech afterwards remain cherished moments. My husband had trained for the catholic priesthood and 10 priests proceeded down the aisle ahead of us including the local bishop who married us. In a very loud stage whisper Dad said to me "One more and we'd have a f====== fitba team!"

He came to London, where Adrian and I had made our home when each of my daughters were born.

Lara, my second daughter was born prematurely with a syndrome and with various life threatening conditions. We were told on three occasions not to expect her to survive. We took her home on full care at 4 months old following a period of time on cardiac intensive care at Great Ormond Street Hospital. Adrian and I had become expert in resuscitating her, managing her oxygen, passing naso gastric tubes etc. Dad flew down on his own to visit us before he himself was admitted for a treatment called brachytherapy. We knew that I would not be able to visit him nor him me for a long time. He told me afterwards that he had prayed that God would take Lara, as he didn't think she would survive. Both of them survived and a special bond existed between them from then on.

The last time I saw him was two weeks before he died. I drove up to Scotland and stayed overnight. He was not awake for long periods but never stayed in bed. He liked to be in the kitchen next to Mum and to be in the middle of all that was going on. It gave me great comfort just to sit and hold his hand and to know that there was nothing left unsaid. All the hurts of the past had been forgiven and we both knew we were loved by the other.

He was and remains one of the most profound influences in my life and as I hear myself repeating his wisdom to my own children, in the lives of the next generation.

The below was 'Thought for the Day' on Fathers day 2003 for BBC Radio Sheffield and my first piece of journalism. It was cathartic for me. It was repeated on Christmas Day as one of the most requested pieces of the year and short listed for a religious broadcast award.

FATHER'S DAY.

Today is father's day, my first without him.

Dad died six weeks ago. Sometimes it feels like an age but mostly it still doesn't feel true.

I still almost pick up the phone to tell him something and have to stop myself asking Mum what kind of night he had, which was my opening line to her at 8.30 every morning for most of the last two years.

His dying days were dark with tension and pain.

His death has released us to remember much better times. We've laughed together and cried together and in some ways he feels more alive now than in the weeks and months before he died.

I miss him.

I miss his hands. They were enormous to me as a child, always warm and dry and amazingly soft for a man who had worked so hard all his life. Hands that played shadow games on my bedroom wall when I was little. Hands that were always a source of comfort and of refuge in the years of adolescence and broken hearts. Hands that held mine when we walked down the aisle at my wedding. Huge hands cradling my newborn babies.

In the last months, when he could no longer talk, he would hold out his hand and we would take turns sitting beside him holding those big warm hands. It always felt like time stood still, a moment of deep peace, an experience of what I believe is God.
On his last morning, he managed to get up and sit next to my mum. He stretched out his hand to her. She took it, he held it, his head fell forward and he was gone. The death we had all prayed for him.

I miss his hands.

I miss my Dad.

Seen by the distinctive view of Hawkeye, the Burnbrae Road depot was opened in 1989. It's now the main Logistics depot serving West Central Scotland, which embraces Ayrshire, Glasgow and Dumbartonshire. There are about 150 staff employed here and it's a base for 65 tractor units. Burnbrae Road is linked to the old Cartside (Johnstone) depot by an internal road and both parts of the complex are now involved in both transit and longer term warehousing.

Pictured in April 2002 by Hawkeye Photography, Malcolm's Fouldubs terminal at Grangemouth is now the centre of the Company's rail-freight network. The terminal is dominated by the 50,000 sq ft transit shed/warehouse while rail sidings – with a total length of 1,200 metres – serve the site. Malcolms currently operate 46 different train journeys with Crick – in the English Midlands – being their most well known destination. However, Malcolms also operate a daily service to Aberdeen and also a regular – five days a week – service to Elderslie, near the Company's HQ at Linwood. Malcolm's Grangemouth Tillyflats warehouse site is on the left of the picture. There are plans to install two further sidings into this site giving an additional 450 metres of siding.

From around 1960, the road going fleet of WH Malcolm began venturing south to England down the A74 and over the f[?]
began their regular rail service to Crick. At 1016' above sea level, the Summit is the highest point on the railway betwe[?]
Rail Services (DRS). This train now operates at a length of 430 metres and conveys up to 30 lorry loads of traffic. Payl[?]
a reflection of the strong link between DRS and the Malcolm Group, the Class 66 diesel electric locomotive – No. 66 [?]
imported to the UK in October 2003. This locomotive frequently hauls the WHM trains between Crick and Grangemou[?]
traffic for Scotland (top left). These modern wagons are liveried in WHM's distinctive colours and were constructed in [?]
59.5 tonnes at a reduced speed of 60mph. The wagons are 23 metres long and have the distinct advantage of a movab[?]
accommodated in each wagon. The Malcolm Group are currently the owners of three of these "Reach Stackers" as seer[?]
and has a lifting capacity of 45 tonnes. The company owns a number of other container lifting machines and a fleet of [?]

Beattock Summit. The route was made easier when upgraded to motorway but from February 2001, the Malcolm Group
on and Glasgow. The train pictured is being hauled by two class 37 locomotives operated by WHM's rail haulier Direct
ound 800 tonnes but the trailing weight (gross weight of the train excluding the locomotive) is around 1,350 tonnes. As
is been painted in Malcolm colours. Constructed by General Motors at their works in London Ontario, Canada it was
as a power rating of 3,300 hp. Two high volume KSA (Talgo) rail wagons stand at Crick awaiting loading with palletised
in 1997. The wagons can run at 75mph with a payload of 51.5 tonnes or if heavier loads are required they can load to
:hat can give a loading height of 2.9 metres which is the best achievable in the UK rail system. Up to 62 Pallets can be
WHM 15S Intermodal Container from a rail wagon (top right). This Reach Stacker was built by the Swedish firm SMV
'00 containers, which are 45' long, 2.5m wide and either 8'9" or 9'6" high.

Compared to the clean-cut image of Logistics, the working conditions of the Malcolm Group's Construction Services Division is rarely clean and hardly pretty. They can however be totally green, as the action (top) at the Merklands site shows how demolition waste is sorted and then re-cycled. Brought onto site by Malcolm vehicles, the material is passed through a crusher where inbuilt magnets, extract all the metal. The material then passes through a wash, allowing any floating timber to be skimmed off. Once crushed to the desired grade, this hard-core type of material is then transported out to be used on other building projects. Jock Brown is believed to be the driver of the Volvo 150 wheeled loader. Merklands was Malcolm's first big re-cycling site, although that operation has now been transferred to the company's South Street site.

The Malcolm Plant gets to all manner of building and construction sites with operator Steve Wilson (lower left) believed to be pictured working on a new supermarket at Kilmarnock. Inserting a main sewer pipe is the above project while the JCB is seen at Gourock overlooking the Firth of Clyde. Malcolms have around 26 of these JCB

machines which are replaced when about two years old. Described as a good reliable machine, they are said to be well liked by their operators. Although the Malcolm machine men are generally allowed just to get on with their job – wherever they are – Eddie Cunningham recalls the day when one of their working machines was given a parking ticket: 'We were working at St Vincent Street in Glasgow and I couldn't believe how the Warden walked inside the fenced off area and slapped a ticket onto the working machine. You never know what's going to happen in this job.'

Through the Years

1923   Walter Hattrick Malcolm and Marion McPhail marry.

1925   Donald Malcolm is born in Johnstone on 16th April.

The Malcolm family move to Boghouse Farm at Brookfield as a base for their new coal round business. Their first horse & cart is put to work.

1930   Walter Malcolm buys his first mechanised load carrier – a Morris 1.5 tonner - for £150.

1934   Walter Malcolm dies in Western Infirmary Glasgow on 28th March at the age of 42. Marion Malcolm continues to run the coal round & contractor business helped by a good friend from the Isle of Lewis – Donald McIver.

1939   After leaving school - at the age of 13 – Donald Malcolm is made a partner, with his mother Marion, in the WH Malcolm business of coal merchant & contractor.

1945   By this time the fleet has increased to five vehicles.

1950   The coal merchant business is sold although delivering coal in bulk is still a major traffic. Contracting work is increased.

1951   The first wheeled mechanical shovel is bought. It's used primarily for loading ash, blaes and rubbish.

1955   The first earth-moving machine is purchased – a Caterpillar 955.

1957   Donald Malcolm and Wilma Buchanan are married at the Grosvenor Hotel in Glasgow on 23rd February.

1958   Donald & Wilma's first child – Wilma Rodger Malcolm - is born on 7th August.

1959   Donald & Wilma's second child – Marion MacPhail Malcolm – is born on 4th December.

1960   Donald & Wilma's third child – Walter Hattrick Malcolm – is born on 9th December.

With a fleet size of 37 vehicles and seven earth-moving machines, WH Malcolm Ltd is formed prior to its acquisition by Grampian Holdings Ltd in November 1960.

William Wilson & Son (Johnstone) Ltd is acquired in December 1960 and at the time is operating 17 vehicles and five earth-moving machines from their Russell Street base.

1961   The long established local carriers concern of Wilson Bros (Haulage) Ltd is acquired with its fleet of 15 vehicles.

1962   Donald & Wilma's fourth child – Andrew Buchanan Malcolm – is born on 13th January.

1964   New offices, workshops and garage are occupied in Murray Street, Paisley in July. The administrative HQ of WH Malcolm Ltd is moved here along with all the tipping vehicles previously based at Brookfield.

The tipper business of John Hutchison & Son (Haulage) Ltd is acquired. 30 vehicles and two earth moving machines are bought in the transaction. However this business is sold back to John Hutchinson in 1971.

In August '64, JL McNeil Ltd of Renfrew is also acquired. This company operates 14 vehicles, most of which are tippers.

The company of Foulis Welding & Engineering Co Ltd (which hires out contractors small plant – compressors, welders, pumps etc) is purchased. This was sold to Scaffolding (GB) Ltd in February 1969.

1965   Tyne Street, Glasgow (Haulage) Ltd is formed to purchase the 26 vehicles & property of John Macdonald (Haulage) Ltd.

Donald Malcolm sells Malcolm Blaes Co.Ltd to Grampian.

Central Garage (Bathgate) Ltd and Russell Motors Ltd are acquired. John Russell continues to manage these companies although these are sold in 1973.

Malcolm Plant Ltd is formed to acquire the business & assets of John Best, which at the time operates six earth-moving machines. All the earth-moving interests of WH Malcolm Ltd are transferred to this new company.

The haulage business and 17 vehicles of Collingwood Engineering Ltd are purchased.

1966   Donald Malcolm buys the 10 strong fleet of James Cunninghame. The licences for these vehicles are upgraded and the bigger (new) vehicles are used on a sub contract basis to the WH Malcolm operation under the Cunninghame name.

1967   The business and 21 vehicles of John Johnstone (Contractors) Ltd are bought. Although premises are also acquired, these are sold and a new depot in Westerburn Street, Shettleston is acquired.

The 26 strong fleet & business of William Kerr (Kilwinning) Ltd is bought.

Donald Malcolm takes 60% and Bill Lind 40% of the newly created Loanhead Transport Ltd. This company is operated as a sub contractor to WH Malcolm Ltd.

1968   A 60% share of Clachan Excavations & Construction Ltd is acquired. However, this share is reduced to 55% within two years when Alex Morton joined the company to stiffen the management.

1969   Because of massive expansion, the general haulage side of the WH Malcolm business is moved from Brookfield to the newly created Cartside depot in Gas Street, Johnstone during November '69. Workshops and offices are also built there.

1970   Fleet size of the WH Malcolm Transport Group now stands at 332 vehicles. Profit has grown from £152,000 in 1961 to £521,000 in 1970.

1972   WH Malcolm establish a presence at Newton le Willows in Lancashire but soon re-locate to premises at Watkin Lane, Lostock Hall, Preston.

Premises are taken at Beacon Services, South Mimms (north of London) to source traffic for the long distance fleet.

1973 The small, Glasgow based, waste disposal concern of Tidysite is acquired primarily to develop the name in the skip moving business.

The Tyne Street depot is closed and this operation moved to a new depot in Castlebank Street, Glasgow.

1974 Marion Malcolm dies on 10th April.

New premises are bought on Nethermains Road, Kilwinning and occupied by vehicles previously based in the ex Kerr depot in the town centre at Woodwynd.

1983 WH Malcolm moves their London depot to Hatfield (these premises are sold in December 2004).

1986 WH Malcolm re-locates their Preston depot to Holme Road, Bamber Bridge.

1989 The premises and seven strong fleet of DAG Transport, Gatenby, North Yorkshire is acquired.

The assets of the Glasgow based LPT Transport are acquired. This consists of 23 vehicles plus 30 plant items, which are distributed around the other Malcolm depots.

Burnbrae Road depot at Linwood is established & developed.

1992 Operational depot at Newhouse started. Originally the premises were rented from Terex but these are purchased on 1.1.96.

1994 Donald Malcolm is voted Personality of the Year by Transport News.

1996 WH Malcolm move into their depot at Haydock in Lancashire.

1997 Malcolm Plant Ltd moves out of Brookfield to Murray Street, Paisley.

The Malcolm Group Burnbrae Drive HQ is opened together with the adjacent Maintenance Services Division.

WH Malcolm opens their Grangemouth depot for road haulage freight use.

1999 The 35 strong fleet of Wilfred Holden of Blackburn in Lancashire is acquired.

2000 WH Malcolm is voted Scottish Haulier of the Year by Transport News.

Express rail freight operation is put into service. Grangemouth and Crick depots opened.

2001 All the vehicles – including trailers - owned by the Malcolm family through the concerns of Loanhead Transport Ltd and Brookfield Securities Ltd are sold to Grampian PLC.

The WH Malcolm depot at Sharpness is opened.

The Grangemouth depot is expanded to also become Malcolm's rail link HQ.

2002 Donald Malcolm is awarded a Lifetime Achievement Award by the Transport News.

2003   Donald Malcolm dies on 3rd May.

Because Grampian PLC's only asset is the Malcolm Group's transport operation, their name is changed to The Malcolm Group PLC.

The road surfacing business of Piries is acquired.

2005   The Malcolm Group PLC is brought back into the ownership of the Malcolm family.

The South Street tipper depot is opened which allows for the centralisation of all the Malcolm tipper & plant operations (apart from those done from Kilwinning).

2006   The company of Charles Lawrence Surfaces Ltd of Newark, Nottinghamshire is acquired. They are a specialist sports surfacing contractor.